mouthwatering
VEGAN

mouthwatering
VEGAN

OVER 130 IRRESISTIBLE RECIPES FOR EVERYONE

MIRIAM SORRELL

PHOTOGRAPHY BY **MIRIAM SORRELL**

appetite
by RANDOM HOUSE

Appetite by Random House and colophon are registered trademarks of Random House of Canada Limited

Library and Archives of Canada Cataloguing in Publication is available upon request

ISBN: 978-0-449-01565-0

Cover image: Miriam Sorrell

Printed and bound in China

Published in Canada by Appetite by Random House,
a division of Random House of Canada Limited

www.randomhouse.ca

10 9 8 7 6 5 4 3 2 1

In loving memory of my late mother, Carmen,

and the late and precious Sr. Alphonsene.

And to my beloved little daughter, Zara.

CONTENTS

INTRODUCTION

made the decision to turn vegan several years ago. I had been brought up in a meat-eating family, and—I won't lie—I loved my meat. But in my early twenties, while living in London, I decided to become vegetarian, and remained so for many years. The more aware I became of where my food came from, the more convinced I became that adopting a vegan diet was the right choice to make, and the logical next step from the beliefs I held as a vegetarian. It was an ethical decision, based on the desire to stop harming animals (see "Why Vegan?" on page 265), and the health benefits of a vegan diet were an added bonus (see "Vegan Nutrition" on page xii).

I have always taken great pleasure in cooking. You could even say that cooking runs through my veins. I grew up in Malta and London, in a food-loving Mediterranean family. My Greek Cypriot father had a successful restaurant in London for many years—where I worked briefly—and I've catered for family and friends for as long as I can remember. I have always enjoyed the creative aspect of cooking: adapting traditional dishes to make my own vegetarian (and later vegan) versions, and experimenting with fusions of different cuisines. I'm fascinated by food and I love stretching the boundaries to explore new territories beyond the obvious. Great food always seems to bring out the best in people. I believe there is a profound sensuality in creating and sharing beautiful food. Taste, color, texture and aroma have to combine in a magical union, which depends on correct cooking methods and times—together with the right blend of ingredients, of course. So, in becoming vegan, I set out to create dishes with that magical quality—dishes that showcase how varied and imaginative vegan food can be. I wanted to come up with vegan versions of much-loved meat- and dairy-based classics that would stand up to—and even improve upon—the traditional versions. I also wanted to create true vegan originals: new, inspired dishes that highlight the flavors and flexibility of plant-based ingredients. I embraced this exciting new challenge with an open mind and heart, filled with passion.

Inspired by the constant encouragement of family and friends, and suggestions that I open a restaurant or write "that cookery book," I started my Mouthwatering Vegan food blog from my home in Malta. My mission was to provide vegans with an array of temptingly delicious dishes, and in so doing attract omnivores and vegetarians alike to this healthier, ethical way of life. I had the vision of presenting virtual dinner guests with the ultimate experience of vegan cooking.

The blog went live in 2010 and I've watched with excitement as it has grown in readership ever since. Before I knew it, I was approached by the New York Vegetarian Food Festival to submit recipes for its brochure. Several food manufacturers asked me to write recipes for them, and publications associated with the Vegan Society wanted to hear from me, too. By the time I was approached to write this book, I'd already started to receive requests from my Facebook followers for a cookbook. My next step was the exciting task of selecting which recipes I would include.

This book is the culmination of many years spent in my kitchen, dedicated to producing the ultimate meat- and-dairy-free cuisine. It encapsulates all that I believe in and hold close to my heart, as well as being a major leap forward in bringing my particular style of vegan cooking to a wider audience. In fact, I would go as far as to describe it as a "meat-free revolution!" The result is a true anthology of vegan cuisine, containing more than 130 recipes that use vegetables from A to Z, fruits familiar and exotic, legumes, herbs, spices, nuts, dried fruits, tofu and a variety of meat substitutes. Whether you are a vegan, a vegetarian, an omnivore or simply a keen foodie, I offer you an abundance of delicious vegan dishes to create and enjoy at home.

I often hear veganism referred to as a lifestyle choice, whereas it is for me a way of life. What I hope to share with you in this book is how worthwhile and fulfilling making the change to veganism can be. If you're already vegan, you know the wonderful rewards of a plant-based diet—both health-wise and heart-wise. If you're not already vegan, changing your way of life and eating habits may appear challenging. Some people have an "aha" moment of awakening to veganism that's so strong it enables them to change their diets instantaneously. But if that's not the case for you, take your time and savor the adventure. After trying a few of my recipes, you'll realize that eating vegan needn't mean sacrificing flavor or beautiful presentation, or missing out on the joys of creative cooking and delicious eating. If you start to include just a few more vegan dishes in your daily diet, then we're both on the right track: eating vegan (even incrementally) is the healthy, nutritious, ethical and ecologically sound choice for all.

So here it is, a collection of more than 130 of my very best vegan recipes to delight your taste buds, keep you in good health and satisfy your soul, while promoting a healthier planet for people and animals alike.

The future, my friends, is vegan!

Miriam Sorrell
MARCH 2013

VEGAN NUTRITION

A vegan diet is one that excludes animal products—such as meat, fish, dairy, eggs and honey—and animal-derived ingredients such as gelatin. (Many vegans also avoid wearing or using animal products, such as leather, fur, wool and silk, and using cosmetics or household products containing animal ingredients.) You may hear criticism that vegan eating does not give the body all that it needs to be healthy, but this is not the case: both the American Dietetic Association and Dietitians of Canada have stated that a well-planned vegan diet is healthful and provides the required nutrients for people at all stages of life.[1]

Vegan and vegetarian diets tend to be higher in fiber, magnesium, potassium, folate and antioxidants, and lower in saturated fat and cholesterol, than diets including meat. As a result, vegans tend to have lower cholesterol and blood pressure, as well as lower rates of heart disease and certain cancers. Eating vegan may also be beneficial for losing weight, or maintaining a healthy weight, without having to "diet." Of course, eliminating animal-based products isn't an automatic key to better health, but a diet based on vegetables, fruits, nuts, seeds, legumes and whole grains—with the occasional indulgence now and then—is highly nutritious.

There are, however, a few nutrients that are more challenging to obtain in a diet without animal products, and it's important to ensure you have a source for them. In their excellent book *Becoming Vegan* (Book

Publishing Company, 2000), Brenda Davis and Vesanto Melina offer a wealth of information and advice on nutritional and dietary considerations for vegans.

Vitamin B12 is the most crucial nutrient that may be difficult to obtain in a completely vegan diet; it is essential for proper functioning of the brain and nervous system, and is found mostly in animal products (plant-based sources are unreliable). Nutritional yeast (see "The Vegan Pantry" section on page xv) is a good vegan source of B12, and some commercial meat substitutes and nondairy milks are fortified with the vitamin also—check the labels on individual products. Many vegans choose to take a B12 supplement, to be sure of getting a regular dose of the vitamin.

A common misconception is that there is a lack of protein in a vegan diet. Actually, it is not difficult to obtain enough protein through vegan foods, so long as you consume a variety of legumes and/or soy foods, nuts, seeds and whole grains on a regular basis. You don't need to worry about "combining" different plant proteins in a single meal; just ensure that you're eating a good variety of these foods as part of your everyday diet.

Vegans and vegetarians also need to be careful to consume foods high in iron, as plant foods do not contain as much absorbable iron as meat or eggs. Good sources of iron include soy and other legumes, greens such as broccoli and spinach, dried fruits, whole grains, nuts, seeds and fortified meat substitutes. Iron from plant sources is less easily absorbed, so to maximize absorption, eat something high in vitamin C at the same time—for example, orange juice or berries with a breakfast cereal of whole grains, dried fruits and nuts, or a salad with beans, greens and tomatoes.

Calcium, a crucial mineral for bone health, is another nutrient vegans should be conscious of eating regularly. Though milk products are traditionally recommended as sources of calcium, there are also excellent nondairy sources of calcium, including leafy green vegetables, almonds, tahini and fortified nondairy milks.

While planning a nutritionally balanced vegan diet may seem a daunting prospect at first, you can find a wealth of information—in books, in natural food stores and online—to guide you as you build your own bank of knowledge.

VEGAN ORGANIZATIONS

Animals Deserve Absolute Protection Today and Tomorrow: **www.adaptt.org**
The Vegan Society: **www.vegansociety.com**
American Vegan Society: **www.americanvegan.org**
Vegan Action: **www.vegan.org**
Vegan Outreach: **www.veganoutreach.org**
People for the Ethical Treatment of Animals: **www.peta.org**

VEGAN PANTRY

BEFORE YOU BEGIN, you'll want to make sure your kitchen is stocked with vegan cooking essentials. Here are the tools and pantry supplies you'll need.

KITCHEN EQUIPMENT

Food processor
A good-quality, powerful food processor is essential for a variety of kitchen tasks, including puréeing, chopping, shredding, grinding and mixing. KitchenAid, Cuisinart and Magimix are excellent brands.

Blender
You'll need a powerful standing blender, such as a VitaMix or KitchenAid, for blending smoothies and chopping hard ingredients like nuts. This is an item where it really pays to invest in quality, as the difference a high-powered blender makes is remarkable.

Handheld immersion blender
A handheld blender is useful for puréeing soups and sauces without having to transfer them from their container.

Juicer
A high-capacity juicer lets you enjoy the myriad benefits of fresh, raw juices. You can put most fruits and vegetables in whole, though citrus fruits need to be peeled first.

Ice-cream maker
You can buy commercial vegan ice creams and sorbets, but it's more fun to make your own. It's not necessary to buy an expensive ice-cream maker—a cheap one will do the job.

Pudding basin
Some of my desserts call for pudding basins, stoneware bowls that come in various sizes. They are inexpensive and available in kitchen stores.

Kitchen scale
A small kitchen scale is helpful for weighing precise amounts of ingredients such as tofu

(when a recipe calls for less than a full package), chocolate or nuts. You can find inexpensive models—either a digital or analog scale will do.

Parchment paper
Parchment paper is useful for lining baking pans; I also use it in my no-bake dessert recipes to avoid sticking and prevent pans from getting scratched.

VEGAN DAIRY

Milk
Commercial nondairy milks come in many flavors and varieties, including soymilk, rice milk, oat milk, coconut milk and nut milk. Different brands vary in thickness, sweetness and taste, so sample a variety to find your preference. Or try making your own (see the recipe for Happy Milk on page 249).

Margarine
Not all brands of margarine are vegan—some contain dairy products—so be sure to read the ingredients. Earth Balance brand is vegan, non-hydrogenated and all natural, and also comes in a soy-free version. Some types of margarine are not suitable for baking, so check the label.

Cheese
For cheese alternatives, see the recipes on pages 252-262 of the Decadent Cheeses & Dairy Alternatives chapter, or look for Daiya, Galaxy, Sheese or Tofutti brands in stores. Some nondairy cheeses contain casein, a milk protein, so check the label to make sure it's vegan.

For a grated hard cheese alternative, you may be able to find packaged grated vegan "Parmesan" alternatives made from soy (look for Parmazano or Galaxy brands) or nuts (Parma! or Parma-Veg), or try my Nutty Parmesan recipe on page 262.

Cream cheese
Tofutti and Galaxy brands make vegan cream cheese, available in tubs in the refrigerator section of natural food stores and some supermarkets. It comes in several flavors (plain, French onion, garlic and herb, etc.) and can be used as a spread or in cooking and baking.

Cream
Many of my recipes call for vegan cream. MimicCreme, a dairy- and soy-free cream substitute made from nuts, is available in some natural food stores, and comes in sweetened and unsweetened versions. You can also make an easy cashew cream that substitutes well for cream in any recipe (see the recipe for Happy Cream on page 249).

Yogurt
Yogurt made from cultured soy, coconut or almond milk is available in dairy sections in a variety of flavors. Use plain soy yogurt for the most neutral flavor in recipes.

GRAINS
I prefer to cook with whole grains, as they contain much more fiber and minerals than refined versions. Among the ones to have on hand are brown rice (short-grain, long-grain and basmati), wild rice, quinoa, barley, millet and rolled oats. In some dishes, where the texture of white rice is preferable, I use short-grain or long-grain white rice, or arborio rice. These grains are all available

in packages or bulk bins in natural food stores and supermarkets.

To cook perfectly fluffy grains, I like to use more water than necessary, then drain and rinse the cooked grain (much like cooking pasta). Here is the basic recipe: Combine 1 cup (250 mL) grain with 3 cups (750 mL) water in a saucepan. Bring to a boil, cover, reduce the heat and simmer until tender (anywhere from 15 to 60 minutes, depending on the type of grain). Drain and rinse in cold water before adding to your recipe.

FLOURS

I use whole wheat flour wherever possible, though where a recipe needs a more refined texture, unbleached all-purpose flour is best. Flours made from brown rice and spelt (a variety of wheat that is often well tolerated by people with wheat allergies) are also good to have on hand. Chickpea flour (sometimes called gram flour), made from ground chickpeas, makes a good binder in burger and sausage recipes. Soy flour, also found in natural food stores, adds protein and moistness to eggless baked goods. Self-rising flour is cake or pastry flour that already has baking powder added; you can substitute 1 cup (250 mL) regular all-purpose flour plus 1½ tsp (7.5 mL) baking powder plus ¼ tsp (1 mL) salt for 1 cup (250 mL) of self-rising flour.

BEANS

Dried beans are inexpensive and easy to prepare, as long as you plan ahead. Some of my favorite varieties are red and brown lentils (which need

no presoaking), split peas, pinto beans and fava beans. Most of my recipes use canned beans: red kidney beans, cannellini (white kidney) beans, chickpeas, lentils and vegan baked beans (check the ingredients, as some canned baked beans include pork). Drain and rinse canned beans before using to reduce the sodium content.

PASTA

Some dried pasta contains eggs, but many varieties are vegan—read the ingredients. I like to use whole wheat pasta wherever possible, but there are many other kinds available; if you're gluten-intolerant, try quinoa or brown rice noodles. Fresh pasta almost always contains eggs, but it is possible to find vegan ravioli or other shapes from specialty pasta makers.

TOFU AND MEAT SUBSTITUTES

There are many commercially available meat substitutes, but be aware that not all are vegan, as some contain egg whites or dairy products. My personal favorites come from the Linda McCartney range, but I would also recommend Gardein, Yves Veggie, Lightlife and Smart Menu brands as alternatives.

Tofu

Tofu is a versatile food that can be used for many different dishes, including scrambled tofu, stir-fries, cheesecake and more. The kind I use most often is firm silken tofu, which blends smoothly for sauces and desserts. Look for Mori-Nu (which comes in Tetra Paks and does not require refrigeration) or Nasoya brands in natural food stores and some supermarkets. You can substitute firm regular tofu in recipes where it is not blended.

Textured vegetable protein (TVP)

Textured vegetable protein, or TVP, is made from defatted soy flour. It is sold dried and can usually be found as granules (to substitute for ground meat in Bolognese sauce, chili, etc.) or as chunks suitable for stews. It must be hydrated before being added to recipes. To hydrate, combine TVP with an equal amount (or slightly less) of hot water or broth in a bowl, and let stand for 5 minutes (it will approximately double in volume). You can also add soy sauce, spices, or other seasonings to the TVP; much like tofu, it will readily absorb the flavors of anything you add to it.

Vegan ground meat substitutes

You can find vegan ground meat substitutes, usually made from soy, in the refrigerator section of most grocery stores. They work well in place of ground beef in many recipes, such as shepherd's pie and Bolognese sauce. You can also substitute crumbled or chopped veggie burgers, or chopped pecans.

Bacon

Some vegetarian "bacon" substitutes contain egg white. Look for vegan varieties from Lightlife or Yves Veggie.

Vegan burgers

There are many varieties of premade vegan burgers, which can usually be found refrigerated or frozen. Some are more "meatlike," while others contain a mixture of grains, nuts or vegetables. Again, many varieties of vegetarian burgers contain eggs or dairy, so read the labels.

Vegan "beef" strips

You can find these in the refrigerator or freezer section of natural food stores and regular grocery stores. They are useful in stews—Gardein and Yves Veggie brands are the best known. If you're avoiding soy, you can substitute seitan (wheat gluten) strips.

NUTS AND SEEDS

Nuts and seeds are an excellent vegan source of protein, minerals and healthy fats, and are important ingredients in many of my recipes. I like to use walnuts, pecans, hazelnuts, pistachios, cashews, almonds, shredded coconut and sunflower seeds.

To toast raw nuts, place them in a dry frying pan over medium–high heat for a few minutes, stirring often, until they're golden brown; alternatively, spread them in a single layer on a baking sheet and roast in a 350°F (180°C) oven for 10–15 minutes, checking frequently so they don't get overbrowned.

OILS

Extra virgin olive oil

Olive oil is my standby for sautéing, frying, drizzling, and salad dressings.

Sunflower oil

I use this light oil for baking, or wherever a more neutral flavor is desired, but you could substitute any other light-tasting oil, such as canola or grapeseed oil.

Sesame oil

This oil, which comes in light and dark (toasted) varieties, adds a nutty flavor to Asian dishes, and works well in stir-fries and Thai curries. Light sesame oil has a higher smoke point than dark, so it is more suitable for deep-frying.

Unsweetened coconut oil
This amazing oil, which is semisolid at room temperature, is excellent for frying, and works well in desserts. The saturated fat it contains has incredible health benefits, unlike the saturated fat found in animal products. Look for an organic, naturally extracted brand.

Flaxseed oil
Flaxseed oil is high in omega-3 fatty acids and makes a great addition to salad dressings and dips. It should not be heated or used for frying, as this alters its chemical composition.

HERBS AND SPICES
I like to cook with a variety of herbs, spices and seasonings. Here are the essentials to have on hand:

- sea salt or Himalayan salt
- coriander (seeds and ground)
- fresh cilantro
- cardamom (seeds and ground)
- cumin (seeds and ground)
- fennel seeds
- turmeric
- curry powder (regular, hot and mild)
- garam masala
- paprika (regular, smoked and sweet)
- crushed red chili pepper flakes
- chili powder
- fresh chilies
- parsley (fresh and dried)
- basil (fresh and dried)

- dried oregano
- dried thyme
- ground cinnamon
- ground nutmeg
- ground allspice
- pumpkin pie spice
- onion powder
- garlic granules and powder
- lemongrass
- fresh ginger
- ground sumac (available in Middle Eastern grocery stores)
- whole peppercorns
- Chinese five-spice powder
- asafoetida powder (available in Indian grocery stores)

BINDERS
Arrowroot powder and cornstarch
Arrowroot (a white powder made from a starchy tuber) and cornstarch can often be used interchangeably for thickening sauces, gravies, puddings and more. Cornstarch turns liquid opaque when mixed, so arrowroot is better suited to clear jellies and sauces.

Agar flakes
Agar is a type of seaweed that is used as a thickener and stabilizer. It is available in both powder and flake forms from natural food stores. I use agar powder in my cheese recipes (pages 252-262). It can also be used to make vegan Jell-O–type desserts, in place of gelatin (which is derived from animal bones): dissolve 1–2 Tbsp (15–30 mL) of agar flakes in 1 cup (250 mL) of fruit juice, simmer until slightly thickened and then chill until set.

Flaxseed

Flaxseed is very high in fiber and omega-3 fatty acids. Ground flaxseed is preferable, as whole flaxseeds tend to pass through the body undigested; you can purchase it ground, or grind whole flaxseeds yourself in a coffee grinder or food processor. Flaxseed can be used as a binder to replace eggs in baking: to replace 1 egg, mix 1 Tbsp (15 mL) ground flaxseed with 3 Tbsp (45 mL) water.

Egg replacer powder

A combination of starches that mimics the leavening and binding properties of eggs in baking. Orgran and Ener-G brands can be found in natural food stores.

SWEETENERS

Sugar

Some brands of refined white sugar and icing sugar sold in North America are not vegan, as cane sugars are often processed using animal bone char (some are not, but it's impossible to tell without contacting the manufacturer). Brown sugar—which is really refined white sugar with added molasses—may also be processed in this way. Try to buy organic sugar, unbleached sugar, raw cane sugar (also called turbinado sugar) or Sucanat (evaporated cane juice). Wholesome Sweeteners and Whole Foods' 365 label are brands to look for. Muscovado sugar is a dark brown sugar with a strong molasses flavor—you can substitute dark brown sugar. Stevia and xylitol are good natural sugar substitutes.

Agave and maple syrup

Agave and maple syrup are the liquid sweeteners I use most often. Agave syrup, or nectar, is a low-glycemic natural sweetener extracted from the agave plant, ideal as an all-purpose sweetener and for sweetening drinks, as it dissolves well. Maple syrup, from the sap of the maple tree, is another natural vegan sweetener prized for its unique flavor. They can often be used interchangeably, or in place of honey. You can also substitute brown rice syrup, barley malt syrup or date syrup, all available from natural food stores.

FLAVORINGS

Nutritional yeast (Engevita brand)

Nutritional yeast is high in vitamin B12, usually found in animal products, making it an important source for vegans of this essential nutrient. The yeast is deactivated, so it's not suitable for baking. The bright yellow flakes have a nutty, cheesy flavor, which makes them an excellent addition to vegan cheese sauces, pastas, scrambled tofu and more. You can find nutritional yeast in bulk in natural food stores.

Vinegar

Vinegar adds tanginess and depth of flavor to food. For salad dressings and seasoning, I use balsamic vinegar or apple cider vinegar. Rice vinegar is good for Asian dishes.

HP Sauce

HP Sauce, or brown sauce, is a traditional condiment made from malt vinegar, tomato, dates, tamarind and spices. It contains no animal ingredients.

Miso

A fermented paste made from soybeans, often combined with rice or other grains, miso is a salty, savory and protein-rich addition to soups, sauces and other dishes. You can buy miso, which comes in varieties ranging from light to dark, in Asian or natural food stores. I prefer the dark variety, which has a richer flavor.

Soy sauce/tamari

Tamari is a naturally fermented soy sauce that adds a deep, complex flavor to many vegan dishes. You can use it interchangeably with regular soy sauce, which is slightly saltier. Gluten-free tamari is also available. Look for tamari in natural food stores or supermarkets.

Teriyaki sauce

A sweet, savory, soy-based sauce used in Asian dishes. I like to make my own (see recipe on page 127), but you can also use a bottled version.

Vegetable stock

Vegetable stock can be purchased as granules, powder or cubes, and adds flavor to soups and sauces. I prefer granules, as they distribute better, but powder or cubes can be substituted. Better Than Bouillon brand produces a vegetarian chicken-flavored stock, useful for "chicken" noodle soup.

Curry paste

For Indian-style curries, I often use tikka or tandoori curry pastes, which are combinations of various Indian spices with oil and other ingredients. Patak's brand is available in Asian stores and in the ethnic food aisles of most supermarkets.

Tahini

Tahini, a paste made from ground sesame seeds, is high in protein and calcium and adds creaminess to dips, dressings and other dishes. You can find it in most grocery stores.

Yeast extract

Marmite and Vegemite are the best-known brands of yeast extract, a salty, slightly bitter black paste that comes in jars and tubes. Some people like it spread on toast, and a little bit adds saltiness and depth of flavor to savory dishes. You'll find it in natural food stores and in some supermarkets.

Sweet chili sauce

Sweet chili sauce is made from chilies and a sweetener. It's a popular condiment in Asian cooking and can be found in Asian grocery stores, and in the ethnic food aisle of supermarkets.

Vegan "fish" sauce

Incredibly, you can buy several brands of vegan "fish" sauce, suitable for flavoring authentic Asian recipes. I use Golden Mountain sauce, available in Asian grocery stores or online through Amazon.com.

Worcestershire sauce

Worcestershire sauce often contains anchovies, so look for vegetarian varieties in natural food stores.

Rosewater, rose essence, rose syrup and rose petals

These add a lovely floral flavor to desserts and savory dishes. You can find rosewater and rose essence (also called rose extract) in natural food stores or natural pharmacies; the essence is much more concentrated. Rose syrup, which is sweetened, is usually available in Indian, Middle Eastern, and Asian grocery stores and in some supermarkets. For fresh rose petals, look for unsprayed roses at farmers' markets or through organic florists. Edible dried rose petals are available in some gourmet food stores and Middle Eastern grocery stores, or find them online through Amazon.com or eBay.

Vegan jelly

Most jelly is made from gelatin, an animal product. For a vegan alternative, try Just Wholefoods Real Fruit brand, available in some natural food stores and through online vegan specialty stores (see below). You can also substitute agar flakes (see page xix).

PASTRY

Puff pastry

Puff pastry is a layered pastry for making light, flaky pie crusts. I find it's too time-consuming to make my own, so I prefer to use a good-quality ready-made brand, such as Aussie Bakery (available at Whole Foods) or Pepperidge Farm.

Phyllo pastry

Made from very thin sheets of dough, phyllo (sometimes called filo) is used in Greek and Middle Eastern pastries, such as baklava. Many brands of phyllo dough are vegan (check the ingredients), and whole wheat and spelt phyllo sheets are also available.

WHERE TO BUY

Depending on where you live, some vegan ingredients can be difficult to find in grocery stores. Here are some online retailers that can help you stock your pantry with vegan essentials and hard-to-find ingredients, including baking supplies, dairy, meat and egg substitutes, and more.

- Karmavore: www.karmavore.ca—ships worldwide
- Vegan Essentials: www.veganessentials.com—ships worldwide
- The Vegan Store: www.veganstore.com—ships within the U.S. and Canada
- Viva Vegan Store: www.vivavegan.ca—ships to Canada and the continental U.S.
- Whole Foods Market: www.wholefoodsmarket.com—online shopping available in some areas; check site for details

BREAKFAST, JUICES & SMOOTHIES

BLACKBERRY MUFFINS MAKES 12 MUFFINS

AN IDEAL QUICK BREAKFAST OR TEATIME PICK-ME-UP, these muffins feature juicy, sweet-tart blackberries in a starring role. They couldn't be simpler to make, and can be thrown together in minutes.

1 cup (250 mL) unbleached all-purpose flour

1 cup (250 mL) self-rising flour (see page xvii)

1 tsp (5 mL) baking soda

1 cup (250 mL) vegan sugar

1 cup (250 mL) nondairy milk (see page 249 or use purchased)

⅓ cup (80 mL) canola or sunflower oil

1 Tbsp (15 mL) apple cider vinegar

a few drops of almond extract

1½ cups (375 mL) fresh or frozen blackberries

1. Preheat the oven to 400°F (200°C). Place 12 paper muffin cups in a nonstick muffin pan.

2. In a large bowl, mix together all the dry ingredients.

3. Combine the wet ingredients (reserving the blackberries) in another bowl, and mix for 30 seconds or so.

4. Slowly pour the wet ingredients into the dry ones, stirring slowly until the ingredients are just blended—don't overmix.

5. Add the blackberries to the batter, and stir gently to distribute them well.

6. Pour the batter into the prepared muffin cups, and pop in the oven for about 20 minutes, until the muffins look golden. Insert a wooden skewer to check that they are ready—it should come out clean.

7. Remove the muffins from the oven and allow them to cool before taking them out of the pan.

8. Now put the kettle on, and serve with a hot cup of tea (removing the muffin papers carefully). Store leftovers in an airtight container.

SCRAMBLED TOFU with Mushrooms

SERVES 4

SCRAMBLED TOFU IS A VEGAN MAINSTAY that's not always very exciting, but this version is truly a masterpiece—once you try it, it will become a brunch-time part of your life forever. The secret is the tahini, which adds a creamy richness and depth of flavor, while turmeric and nutritional yeast turn the tofu an egglike yellow. The 3-Layered Breakfast Toast variation below was inspired by a great hunger for an extra-delectable Sunday brunch, with layers of vegan sausage, baked beans, scrambled tofu and melted vegan cheese . . . mmm! Serve with a Banana, Oat & Cinnamon Smoothie (see the recipe on page 17) to round out the meal.

---

olive oil

1 large red onion, chopped

4 large cloves garlic, chopped

2½ tsp (12.5 mL) grated fresh ginger

8 medium mushrooms, chopped

2 12.3-oz (349-g) packages firm silken tofu

4 Tbsp (60 mL) soy sauce

1 tsp (5 mL) dried oregano, or 4 tsp (20 mL) chopped fresh oregano

1 tsp (5 mL) nutritional yeast (optional)

2 tsp (10 mL) turmeric

4 Tbsp (60 mL) tahini

1. Heat a drizzle of olive oil in a nonstick frying pan set over medium heat, then sauté the onion until transparent.

2. Add the garlic, ginger and mushrooms and cook for another minute, stirring every few seconds.

3. Crumble the tofu into the pan (then quickly rinse your hands), and stir for a minute or so. Stir in the soy sauce, then add the rest of the ingredients and cook for another minute, stirring.

4. Serve immediately with whole-grain toast and a glass of freshly squeezed orange juice.

VARIATION: 3-LAYERED BREAKFAST TOAST
SERVES 1

Prepare the scrambled tofu as above and keep it warm, then toast 3 slices of bread and spread them with vegan margarine. Spread the first piece of toast with mustard, and top with slices of cooked vegan sausage and heated vegan baked beans. Top with another slice of toast, some grated vegan cheese and some scrambled tofu, and finish with the last piece of toast. Then munch your way to culinary delight!

SPANISH-STYLE OMELETTE

SERVES 4 (MAKES 2 LARGE OMELETTES)

AT LONG LAST, VEGANS NEED NOT FEEL DEPRIVED AT BRUNCH! This sublime omelette, made with blended silken tofu and filled with sautéed veggies and vegan mozzarella, looks remarkably like eggs, and has a lovely texture and flavor. It's a delicious meal in itself, suitable for breakfast, lunch or dinner.

olive oil

1 small zucchini, diced small

¼ red bell pepper, diced small

1 small red or Spanish onion, finely chopped

6–8 brown mushrooms, finely chopped

1 potato, cooked and diced small

7 oz (200 g) firm silken tofu

¼ tsp (1 mL) turmeric

¼ tsp (1 mL) garlic granules

salt to taste (see note)

3 Tbsp (45 mL) nutritional yeast

¾ cup (185 mL) soymilk or other nondairy milk (see page 249 or use purchased)

1½ tsp (7.5 mL) tahini

3 Tbsp (45 mL) unbleached all-purpose flour or gluten-free flour (see note)

4 slices Vegan Mozzarella (see page 253 or use purchased), chopped into 2-inch (5-cm) pieces, or about 1½ cups (375 mL) grated

1. Heat a drizzle of oil in a saucepan and gently sauté the vegetables (including the cooked potato) for a few minutes, until slightly golden and crisp. Set them aside for filling the omelettes.

2. To make the batter, combine the remaining ingredients except the cheese in a bowl. Using a handheld immersion blender or mixer, blend until thick and creamy. Taste and add more salt if needed. The batter will be quite thick—this is necessary for binding the omelette. Don't be tempted to add more liquid.

3. Heat an oiled nonstick frying pan for 1–2 minutes, then add half the batter with a soup ladle. Cook for 1 minute. Add half the cheese overtop and cook for another 3–4 minutes, gently working a spatula under the edges to keep the omelette from sticking.

4. Spread half the cooked vegetables evenly on top of the cheese, and allow to cook for 3–4 minutes.

5. Carefully fold the omelette in half, making sure it is not stuck to the pan. Gently tuck the spatula under the folded omelette, and use the pan (not the spatula) to slide it onto a plate—it should slide off fairly easily.

6. Repeat with the remaining batter, cheese and filling to make the second omelette. Serve with your favorite breakfast accompaniments.

NOTE: Try substituting the salt with *kala namak* (black salt), available from Indian grocery stores—it adds a slightly sulfurous, eggy flavor. If you wish to make this recipe gluten-free, you can use a packaged gluten-free flour, or combine equal parts tapioca, rice and corn flours. Remember that the denser you want the texture to be, the more flour you will have to add.

CASHEW & LEEK QUICHE SERVES 4

THIS IS NO ORDINARY QUICHE. It was partly inspired by a dish I had many years ago when I was studying holistic medicine in college, where they served delectable vegetarian food. It's ideal for picnics, brunches, lunches or as a dinner entrée with a salad of fresh red pepper, shredded carrot, cherry tomato and red onion—a memorable feast to relish!

PASTRY

½ cup (125 mL) unbleached all-purpose flour

½ cup (125 mL) whole wheat flour

¼ cup (60 mL) vegan margarine

a pinch of salt

2–3 Tbsp (30–45 mL) cold water

FILLING AND ASSEMBLY

1 large leek, sliced

2½ tsp (12.5 mL) egg replacer powder (see page xx) combined with 1 Tbsp (15 mL) water

1 cup (250 mL) vegan cream (see page 249 or use purchased)

½ cup (125 mL) soymilk

fine sea salt to taste

1 cup (250 mL) chopped or grated vegan cheese that melts—use either Vegan Mozzarella (see page 253), Mild Cheddar "Cheese" (see page 254) or purchased

a few basil leaves, roughly chopped

¾ cup (185 mL) whole raw cashews

extra virgin olive oil, for drizzling

1 tsp (5 mL) ground nutmeg

PASTRY

1. Place all the ingredients except the water in the food processor and process until you have a consistency similar to that of breadcrumbs.

2. Transfer into a large mixing bowl and slowly add the water, while kneading the mixture with your hands, until a ball is formed.

3. Dust the ball with flour, place in a plastic bag and refrigerate for an hour or so.

4. Grease a 9-inch (23-cm) quiche pan or pie plate. On a clean surface dusted with flour, roll out the pastry to fit the pan. Carefully transfer the pastry to the pan, trimming off any extra around the edge.

TO ASSEMBLE

1. Preheat the oven to 400°F (200°C).

2. Steam the leek slices in a vegetable steamer until soft. Distribute them evenly over the pastry base in the quiche pan.

3. Combine the egg replacer and water mixture with the vegan cream, soymilk and salt in a medium bowl. Using a handheld immersion blender (or a whisk), blend or whisk until smooth, then pour over the leeks.

4. Distribute the chopped cheese evenly over the top, followed by the basil leaves, cashews, a pinch of salt and a drizzle of olive oil. As a last touch, sprinkle on the nutmeg.

5. Bake in the preheated oven for about 40 minutes, until golden. Make sure the quiche has fully set—if not, leave in the oven for a few more minutes.

6. Remove from the oven and allow it to cool for a few minutes before slicing and serving. It also tastes great when served cold.

SIZZLE-SOZZLE SAUSAGES

MAKES 8 SAUSAGES

THE GOOD OLD BREAKFAST SAUSAGE is something many of us enjoyed as kids. It's not particularly healthy in its original meat form, and definitely not animal-friendly, but this vegan version is both, and certainly worth the effort. Serve at breakfast with pancakes or scrambled tofu, or at dinner with vegetables or salad—kids love them too. For best results, make the sausages a day before cooking them.

---

1 green apple, peeled, cored and roughly chopped

6 slices vegan bacon, roughly chopped

1 14-oz (398-mL) can red kidney beans, drained and rinsed

2 tsp (10 mL) ground flaxseed

1½ cups (375 mL) white breadcrumbs, very coarsely processed

¾ cup (185 mL) mixed nuts (blanched almonds, walnuts, cashews), finely chopped

1 onion, very finely chopped

2 cloves garlic, finely chopped

1½ Tbsp (22.5 mL) chickpea (gram) flour (see page xvii)

1 Tbsp (15 mL) mixed fresh herbs (parsley, rosemary and sage work well)

½ tsp (2 mL) onion powder or flakes

¼ tsp (1 mL) coriander seeds

¼ tsp (1 mL) smoked paprika (optional)

¼ tsp (1 mL) chili powder

salt to taste

1. Place the apple in a saucepan with a little water and stew for about 15 minutes, until cooked. Drain and set aside.

2. Pulse the vegan bacon a few times in your food processor until finely chopped.

3. Add the kidney beans to the food processor with the bacon, and process until the beans have broken down to a thick consistency.

4. Add the remaining ingredients and pulse a few times again.

5. Finally, add the stewed apple and process until the mixture is a thick, pulpy consistency.

6. Spoon into a large bowl and refrigerate for at least 1 hour. If time is not on your side, place in the freezer for 20 minutes instead.

7. Divide the mixture into 8 portions and shape each portion into a ball in your palms. Then, using either a large cutting board or a clean work surface, roll out each ball into the shape of a sausage. Place on a floured, cooled plate. Cover and refrigerate for several hours, or preferably overnight, before frying.

8. Before cooking the sausages, preheat the oven to 300°F (150°C). Heat a little olive oil in a large frying pan over medium heat, and fry the sausages, turning them carefully, until golden on all sides. Transfer to a baking sheet and place in the preheated oven for 20 minutes before serving.

SPICY SAUCY SAUSAGES

MAKES 8 SAUSAGES

THIS IS A VERY SAUCY AND SLIGHTLY SPICY BRITISH-STYLE SAUSAGE, ideal as part of a full English breakfast, or at dinner with your favorite mustard, vegetables and crunchy bread. My Teriyaki Sauce (see the recipe on page 127) makes the sausages flavorful and moist, but you can substitute a bottled version.

---

1 7-inch (18-cm) white baguette, coarsely torn into chunks

a handful of fresh flat-leaf parsley

4 cloves fresh garlic

1 14-oz (398-mL) can pinto beans, drained and rinsed

2 tsp (10 mL) ground flaxseed

2½ Tbsp (37.5 mL) ketchup

⅓ red bell pepper, finely chopped

½ small onion, finely chopped

¼ tsp (1 mL) ground nutmeg

4 tsp (20 mL) thick teriyaki sauce (see page 127 or use purchased)

1 tsp (5 mL) fresh thyme or ¾ tsp (4 mL) dried thyme

2 tsp (10 mL) garlic granules

2½ tsp (12.5 mL) unbleached all-purpose flour

olive oil

1. Place the baguette in a food processor and process until you have coarse crumbs. Transfer to a large plastic bowl.

2. Process the parsley and garlic in the food processor for 30 seconds.

3. Add the pinto beans and flaxseed and process until the beans are roughly broken down, using a spatula to scrape down the sides of the processor.

4. Add the ketchup and process for a few more seconds—it is important that your mix doesn't resemble mashed potatoes in consistency, so process just enough to break the ingredients down, without making them mushy. Scoop this mixture into the bowl with the breadcrumbs.

5. Add the chopped red pepper, onion and the rest of the ingredients to the bowl and mix together.

6. Divide the mixture into 8 equal portions and shape each portion into a ball in your hands. Roll each ball out into a sausage shape on a clean surface. Place the sausages in a dish and refrigerate for at least 1 hour (or up to 2 days) before frying.

7. To fry, heat a little olive oil for 1 minute in a frying pan set over medium heat. Add the sausages and cook, turning, until all sides have turned golden.

8. Serve immediately, or allow to cool, and reheat in the oven when you wish.

BLOOD PURIFIER SERVES 2

CLEANSE YOURSELF FROM THE INSIDE OUT with this delicious combination of beet, apples, grapes and ginger—it'll get your cells circulating in the right direction and fill you with renewed health and vitality.

1 large beet

3 red apples

1 1-inch (2.5-cm) piece fresh ginger (no need to peel)

2 cups (500 mL) red grapes

2–3 fresh mint leaves, for garnish

1. Cut the beet and apples into pieces small enough to fit in your juicer.

2. Feed the ingredients through the juicer, pour into glasses and garnish with mint leaves.

BLOOD ORANGE & GREENS JUICE

SERVES 2

BLOOD ORANGE, BROCCOLI, LEMON, GRAPES, CELERY AND GINGER come together to bring you and your cells some inner sunshine. Sip immediately after juicing in order to gain the full health benefits of the fruits and vegetables and their live enzymes.

1 blood orange, peeled

1 cup (250 mL) broccoli florets

1½ cups (375 mL) green or red grapes

1 stalk celery

1 1-inch (2.5-cm) piece fresh ginger (no need to peel)

1 lemon, peeled

1. Feed all the ingredients through your juicer.

2. Pour into glasses and drink immediately.

THE REAL THING SERVES 2

THIS AWESOME DRINK WAS INSPIRED in part by the contents of my fridge, and in part by the cleansing benefits of cucumbers and grapes. It really is "The Real Thing" for energizing you, filling you with vitality and enhancing your well-being—plus, the taste is sublime.

3 green apples, cut to fit juicer

2 stalks of celery

1 1-inch (2.5-cm) piece fresh ginger

about 30 grapes

1 orange, peeled

1 large cucumber, cut to fit juicer

1. Run all the ingredients through your juicer.

2. Pour into glasses, sip and enjoy!

NOTE: Always use fresh, refrigerated and washed fruit and vegetables for all your juices and smoothies.

SUNBLAST CELL REJUVENATOR

SERVES 2

PACKED WITH BETA CAROTENE, AMONG OTHER SUPER-NUTRIENTS, this juice not only tastes amazing, but looks amazing, too. Enjoy it!

1 mango, peeled and sliced

1 medium carrot

2 cups (500 mL) fresh pumpkin or other winter squash, peeled and chopped

1 orange, peeled

just under 1 cup (250 mL) cold water

ice cubes or crushed ice

1. Run all the fruits and vegetables through your juicer.

2. Stir in the water and pour into ice-filled glasses. Drink the sublime nectar at once, in small sips.

YOUTH IN A GLASS SERVES 2

PACKED WITH POWERFUL ANTIOXIDANTS and full of vitamins and minerals, this juice takes some beating. In addition to being a natural diuretic, beneficial for kidney function, its nutrients can aid weight loss, clear skin and prevent DNA damage, which leads to signs of aging—hence its title!

1 cup (250 mL) green grapes

2 green apples, cut to fit juicer

2 cups (500 mL) broccoli stems and florets, chopped

2 stalks celery

squeeze of fresh lemon juice

1 tsp (5 mL) wheatgrass powder

1. Run all the fruits and vegetables through your juicer.

2. Add the lemon juice and wheatgrass powder. Mix well with a fork or small hand whisk, then sip and enjoy.

NOTE: Wheatgrass powder is available in natural food stores.

BLUEBERRY & BANANA SMOOTHIE SERVES 2

ENRICHED WITH ANTIOXIDANTS (from the berries) and potassium (from the banana), this is a chill-out delicious smoothie that can be enjoyed by kids and adults alike.

1 frozen ripe banana

¾ cup (185 mL) frozen blueberries

3 frozen strawberries

1 cup (250 mL) chilled water

1. Combine all the ingredients in a blender and blend until smooth.

2. Pour into chunky glasses and sip, or if it's really thick, scoop with a spoon!

BANANA, OAT & CINNAMON SMOOTHIE SERVES 2

THIS SHAKE IS DELIGHTFULLY FULL-FLAVORED, chilled and ever-so-crazy with deliciousness. It's a weekly Sunday-morning treat in my house, and one you'll want to repeat again and again, too.

1 ripe frozen banana

1 cup (250 mL) nondairy milk (see page 249 or use purchased)

1–2 Tbsp (15–30 mL) agave or maple syrup

3–4 ice cubes

2 Tbsp (30 mL) rolled oats

2 Tbsp (30 mL) raw blanched almonds

1 tsp (5 mL) ground cinnamon

1 cup (250 mL) cold water

1. Place all the ingredients except the water in a blender and blend until smooth.

2. Add the water and blend again. Make sure there are no lumps, and that it's nice and frothy on top. If it seems too thick, add a little more milk or water and blend again. Pour and enjoy!

FIGS & ROSES SMOOTHIE SERVES 2

OF ALL THE FRUITS IN EXISTENCE, figs are at the top of my list. Every summer I gorge myself with them, make desserts with them and include them in my salads. But I had never tasted them in a smoothie before coming up with this incredible combination, and now I know I was missing out! Try it; you won't be disappointed.

½ frozen ripe banana

4 fresh figs

1 tsp (5 mL) rose syrup (see page xxi)

5 ice cubes

drizzle of maple syrup (optional)

a few drops of rose essence

a few drops of natural red food coloring (optional)

a pinch of crushed cardamom seeds

1 cup (250 mL) ice-cold water

coconut cream or vegan cream (see page 249 or use purchased), for garnish (optional)

1. Place all the ingredients except the cream in a blender, reserving ½ cup (125 mL) of the water, and blend until smooth.

2. Add the rest of the water and pulse a few times.

3. Pour into glasses, and top with a little coconut cream or other vegan cream, if desired.

ROSE, COCONUT & CARDAMOM SMOOTHIE SERVES 2

I NOT ONLY LOVE ROSES—their smell, their color and their romance—I love their flavor, too. If you adore roses as I do, you will fall in love with this creamy, exotic creation. For an extra nice touch, garnish with fresh rose petals, if you have them on hand.

1 cup (250 mL) thick coconut milk, chilled

2 tsp (10 mL) solid unsweetened coconut oil

2 Tbsp (30 mL) agave or maple syrup

2 tsp (10 mL) natural rosewater (see page xxi)

6 ice cubes

¼ cup (60 mL) vegan cream (see page 249 or use purchased)

¼ tsp (1 mL) ground cardamom (or more to taste)

1½ Tbsp (22.5 mL) rose syrup

¾ cup (185 mL) ice-cold water

fresh rose petals, for garnish (optional)

1. Place all the ingredients except the rose petals in a blender and blend until smooth, frothy and creamy. Pour into glasses and garnish with rose petals, if desired.

APPETIZERS & SIDES

MY GREEK FAMILY TREE
HUMMUS SERVES 4

HAVING GREEK BLOOD, I've tasted just about every hummus around. This version is a family recipe that I spent years tweaking to perfection. Let me preach no longer, and allow this heavenly dip to reach your palate swiftly and surely.

2 cloves garlic

1 14-oz (398-mL) can chickpeas, drained and rinsed

1½ Tbsp (22.5 mL) raw tahini

juice of 1 lemon

3–4 Tbsp (45–60 mL) extra virgin olive oil

salt to taste (this is a key ingredient, so don't omit unless you have to)

4 Tbsp (60 mL) water, or more, depending on desired consistency

1. Place the garlic in a food processor and process until very finely chopped.

2. Add the chickpeas and continue to process until well broken down.

3. Add the tahini and process further.

4. Add the lemon juice, oil and salt. Continue to process, adding the water bit by bit, until a thick paste is formed.

5. If you wish to have a thinner consistency, gradually add more water, a little at a time, until you are happy with the texture. It ought to be smooth (and a little runny, in my opinion).

6. Decant into a small serving bowl, place a black olive in the middle and drizzle with olive oil.

7. Cover and refrigerate, then serve with a Greek salad and warm pita bread.

SPICY GREEK & INDIAN PINTO BEAN DIP SERVES 4

I MADE THIS RECIPE AS AN EXPERIMENT to combine my love of Indian food with my Greek origins—and it worked! Who would have thought pinto beans would taste so delicious combined with Indian spices and the Greek flavors of lemon, mint and tahini? Serve as a dip, or as part of an Indian meal with poppadoms and your favorite curry. This mixture is also delicious as a sandwich filling, or better still, in a ciabatta with lettuce, cucumber and thinly sliced tomatoes.

10 fresh mint leaves or 2 Tbsp (30 mL) chopped fresh cilantro

4 large cloves garlic

1 14-oz (398-mL) can pinto beans, drained and rinsed

½ tsp (2 mL) crushed red chili pepper flakes

3 Tbsp (45 mL) flaxseed oil

1 Tbsp (15 mL) tahini

juice of 1 lemon

2 tsp (10 mL) apple cider vinegar

½ tsp (2 mL) cumin seeds

salt to taste

½ tsp (2 mL) ground cardamom

olive oil, for drizzling

1. Place the mint and garlic in a food processor and process until finely chopped.

2. Add the pinto beans and chili flakes, and process until smooth.

3. Add the remaining ingredients except the cardamom and olive oil and continue to blend for 1–2 minutes, until thick and smooth.

4. Transfer to a bowl, sprinkle with the ground cardamom and round off with a drizzling of olive oil. Cover and refrigerate for several hours before serving.

MOROCCAN SMOKED EGGPLANT DIP SERVES 4

THIS IS ONE OF MY FAVORITE DIPS—flavorful, versatile, yummy and satisfying. The smokiness of the eggplant is ever so addictive. If you want a spicier version, add a little chili powder. Serve as a dip with pita bread or crackers, in a sandwich or wrap, or alongside Exotic Stuffed Artichokes (see the recipe on page 170) for a main meal.

---

1 medium eggplant

3 Tbsp (45 mL) olive oil, plus extra for drizzling

2 cloves garlic, very finely chopped

1 tsp (5 mL) sweet paprika

½ tsp (2 mL) ground cumin

salt to taste (it will need it)

juice of ½ small lemon

freshly ground black pepper to taste

1. Wash the eggplant and then, using a roasting fork (or other long fork) stuck into its side, hold it over an open flame or gas stove, turning it frequently to scorch and blacken it. Once the eggplant is entirely scorched and wrinkled, place it in a large bowl and allow to cool.

2. When the eggplant is cool enough to handle, peel off the black skin and discard (you may need a bowl of water next to you to wash your fingers, as this is a sticky operation).

3. Place the flesh in a bowl and mash it until you have a nice, thick pulp.

4. Heat the olive oil in a saucepan set over medium–low heat and fry the garlic, spices and salt for 1 minute, then add the mashed eggplant, lemon juice and pepper. Cook the mixture for a few minutes, mixing and mashing it further, until it takes on a deep orange color. Transfer to a bowl.

5. Smooth the mixture with a fork and drizzle some olive oil on top.

6. Allow to cool, then cover and refrigerate for several hours before serving.

NOTE: **You will need an open flame or gas stove for this recipe.**

BIGILLA SERVES 4

BIGILLA is a traditional Maltese pâté made with fava beans (also called broad beans)—the "steak" of the legume world. It's rich, filling, nutritious and so easy to make. Spread on crusty bread, it makes an excellent starter or light summer meal. It's also magical as a pizza topping. Note that this recipe uses dried beans, so you'll need to plan ahead.

5 oz (150 g) dried fava beans (about ¾ cup/185 mL)

2 cloves garlic

3 sprigs fresh flat-leaf parsley, leaves and top half of stems

2 Tbsp (30 mL) apple cider or white wine vinegar

2 Tbsp (30 mL) sunflower oil

salt to taste

a pinch of freshly ground black pepper (optional)

olive oil, for drizzling

1. Soak the beans overnight in plenty of water.

2. Drain and rinse the beans, then place them in a pot and cover with fresh water. Bring to a boil, reduce the heat and simmer until the beans are tender and their skins begin to break apart, about 1½ hours. Top up the water as necessary while cooking. Allow the beans to cool, rinse and drain them and set aside in a bowl.

3. In a food processor, process the garlic cloves and parsley until finely chopped.

4. Add the beans and process until well mashed.

5. Add the vinegar, oil, salt and pepper (if using) and process until smooth. The texture will not be perfectly smooth because of the bean skins, but this doesn't matter (in fact, traditionally, bigilla is roughly mashed).

6. Transfer the pâté to a bowl and smooth out with a spatula. Pour a little olive oil on top, cover and refrigerate. It will stay fresh in the fridge for several days.

7. Serve with crackers or bread, or on a hot ciabatta spread with tomato paste, with a drizzle of olive oil and sprinkle of fresh parsley on top.

PECAN & COGNAC PÂTÉ SERVES 4

THIS MOUTHWATERING CREATION CROPPED UP in my mind late one winter's night—
I suppose subconsciously I was rustling up ideas for the festive season. The combination of
buttery roasted pecans with cognac and herbs produces a scrumptious result.

olive oil

2 cups (500 mL) pecan halves

4 slices whole-grain bread

4 cloves garlic

4 sprigs fresh flat-leaf parsley

2 fresh sage leaves (optional)

2 Tbsp (30 mL) vegan margarine

4 Tbsp (60 mL) extra virgin olive oil

salt to taste

4 Tbsp (60 mL) cognac

pinch of freshly ground black pepper
(optional)

1. Gently fry the pecans in a little olive oil for a few minutes, or place them on a baking sheet and roast for 10 minutes in a 400°F (200°C) oven, then set aside.

2. Cut the crusts off the bread slices and discard, dip the slices in a bowl of water, squeeze out any excess and set aside for step 4.

3. In a food processor, place the toasted nuts, garlic, parsley and sage (if using) and process to a fine consistency. Use a spatula to scrape down the sides as necessary.

4. Add the margarine, moistened bread, olive oil and salt and process for 1 minute. Add the cognac and pepper (if desired) and process again for another minute.

5. Transfer to a bowl and serve with raw vegetables, crackers, whole-grain toast wedges or pita bread.

CHILI OLIVE, GARLIC & ROSEMARY BRUSCHETTA SERVES 4

THIS CRUSTY, TASTY BREAD WAS CREATED to pair with the Mediterranean flavors of my Greek Garlic Bean Stew (see the recipe on page 153), but it's an excellent accompaniment to almost any soup or dip. Simple and effective, it takes minutes to prepare, and it's spicy enough to blow away the cobwebs on chilly days.

2 baguettes, or an Italian-style bread, such as ciabatta

4 cloves garlic, finely chopped

15 chili green olives, chopped (see note)

extra virgin olive oil, for drizzling

2 Tbsp (30 mL) fresh rosemary

salt to taste

1. Preheat the oven to 400°F (200°C).

2. Slice the bread into pieces ¾ inch (2 cm) thick and place them on a baking sheet.

3. Sprinkle each slice with chopped garlic and, using a teaspoon, distribute the chopped olives evenly on top.

4. Drizzle the slices with olive oil and sprinkle with the rosemary and salt.

5. Place in the oven for about 12 minutes, until slightly browned.

6. Serve on its own, as an accompaniment to stew or soup, or with a dip or spread.

NOTE: Chili green olives are olives that have been marinated with spices and hot peppers. You can usually find them in delis or your grocery store olive bar. If you can't find them, combine 1 tsp (5 mL) tomato paste with a sprinkle of crushed red chili pepper flakes, a little salt and a drizzle of olive oil, then toss with cracked Mediterranean-style green olives.

ROSEMARY GARLIC BREAD

SERVES 2 OR 3 (DEPENDING ON HOW PASSIONATE YOU ARE)

THIS GARLIC BREAD IS SCRUMPTIOUS, delicious, crunchy and heavenly. What could be better than fresh herbs on freshly baked baguette, topped with extra virgin olive oil, lots of freshly chopped garlic and a pinch of sea salt? This makes a great accompaniment to just about any soup, pasta or main dish.

1–2 fresh baguettes (don't buy ones that are well done, as you will be baking them further)

10 cloves garlic, finely chopped

1 bunch fresh rosemary leaves, chopped

18 fresh basil leaves, chopped

1–2 Tbsp (15–30 mL) extra virgin olive oil (don't skimp on this)

a pinch of salt

1. Preheat the oven to 400°F (200°C) and grease a nonstick baking sheet.

2. Cut the bread into slices roughly ½ inch (1 cm) thick, and place them on the prepared sheet.

3. Place the garlic in a bowl with the herbs, olive oil and salt, and stir well.

4. Using a teaspoon, spread a little of the mixture on each bread slice, distributing as equally as possible.

5. Place in the hot oven for about 12 minutes, until the edges of the bread take on a slight golden color, then serve immediately.

MEDITERRANEAN-STYLE TOMATOED BREAD SERVES 4

THIS IS ONE OF THE SIMPLEST RECIPES YOU WILL EVER MAKE, and one of the most gratifying. Here in Malta, nearly everyone eats this as a staple part of their diet in the summer. We love it as an accompaniment to any salad, or simply by itself. Serve with salty black olives on the side.

---

4 ripe beefsteak tomatoes

8 slices ciabatta or other crusty bread

2 Tbsp (30 mL) sunflower oil, drizzled on a flat plate for dipping

salt and freshly ground black pepper to taste

1. Slice the tomatoes in half horizontally, then smear them on the bread, using 1 tomato half per slice of bread.

2. Dip the tomatoed bread in the oil, then place any leftover tomato bits on the bread.

3. Add a sprinkle of salt and pepper and, hey, presto, there you have it!

NOTE: You MUST find good, flavorful, ripe tomatoes for this—otherwise don't bother. Also, this recipe doesn't work as well with whole-grain bread, so this is one of those times when you must let yourself off the hook and go for a white ciabatta or other Mediterranean-style bread.

WINNER CORNBREAD

SERVES 6–8 (MAKES ONE 9-INCH/23-CM ROUND PAN)

FOND MEMORIES OF MY AMERICAN CHILDHOOD FRIENDS prompted me to have a go at making my own cornbread. This combination of ingredients was an outright winner—not much of it remained the next day. It makes a terrific accompaniment for chili (see the recipe on page 150) or soup.

1 Tbsp (15 mL) egg replacer powder (see page xx)

4 Tbsp (60 mL) water

1 cup (250 mL) cornmeal

1 cup (250 mL) self-rising flour (see page xvii)

¼ cup (60 mL) vegan sugar

1 tsp (5 mL) baking powder

½ tsp (2 mL) salt

1 cup (250 mL) soymilk

⅓ cup (80 mL) sunflower oil

½ small green bell pepper, finely chopped

1. Preheat the oven to 375°F (190°C) and grease a 9-inch (23-cm) pie plate with vegan margarine or oil.

2. In a small bowl, combine the egg replacer powder with the water, stirring to remove any lumps.

3. Combine all the dry ingredients in a large mixing bowl.

4. Add the soymilk, sunflower oil and egg replacer mixture and stir well.

5. Stir in the chopped green pepper.

6. Pour the batter into the prepared pie plate and bake for about 25 minutes.

7. Check to see if the cornbread is cooked by inserting a wooden skewer into the center—if it's clean when you take it out, the cornbread is ready. Cut into wedges and serve.

SMOKED CAPONATA SERVES 4

THIS IS BASED ON A RATATOUILLE SAUCE, but it is more concentrated and richer in flavor. It works well as a topping for baked potatoes, and it's great with pasta. Served on a platter around a whole, steamed cauliflower, it makes an impressive centerpiece. I like to serve it on top of crispy wok-fried potatoes in their skins, with a side salad of cannellini beans tossed with lemon, parsley, olive oil and garlic.

4 Tbsp (60 mL) extra virgin olive oil, plus extra as needed

1 medium eggplant, cubed

2 medium zucchini, chopped

1 medium onion, finely chopped

7 cloves garlic, finely chopped

¾ tsp (4 mL) fennel seeds

¾ tsp (4 mL) coriander seeds

1½ tsp (7.5 mL) smoked paprika

1½ Tbsp (22.5 mL) tomato paste

about 10 black olives

3 cups (750 mL) fresh or canned chopped tomatoes (about 1½ lb/ 750 g)

salt to taste

1. Heat the oil in a nonstick saucepan set over medium heat. Fry the eggplant until lightly brown, stirring from time to time.

2. Add the zucchini and cook, stirring, until it starts to color.

3. Add the onion and garlic, and continue to cook for 3 or 4 minutes, stirring frequently, until they have softened.

4. Stir in the fennel and coriander seeds, and cook for a couple of minutes.

5. Add the smoked paprika. Stir again, cover, reduce the heat to low and cook for 1 minute.

6. Add the tomato paste and cook for another 5 minutes.

7. If your pan is a little dry, add some more olive oil. Add the olives and chopped tomatoes and season cautiously with salt (if your olives are salty, you may not need much). Lower the heat to minimum and simmer for 15 minutes.

FOREVER GIARDINIERA

MAKES ABOUT 4 CUPS (1 L)

THE FLAVOR AND AROMA OF THIS RECIPE bring back many nostalgic memories of my childhood at the beach in Malta, where *giardiniera*—a Mediterranean dish of pickled vegetables—was a summertime staple. My version, with the addition of eggplant and sundried tomatoes, is somewhere between a giardiniera and a caponata, and simply mouthwatering. Eat it with ciabatta bread or as a delicious pizza topping with vegan cheese.

4 Tbsp (60 mL) extra virgin olive oil, plus extra for sealing

1 small eggplant, diced into about 1-inch (2.5-cm) cubes

1 onion, thinly sliced into rings

2 stalks celery, chopped

3 red bell peppers, sliced lengthwise into wide strips

2 green bell peppers, sliced lengthwise into wide strips

1 carrot, grated

2–3 cloves garlic, slivered

1 large green chili, chopped

1½ tsp (7.5 mL) coriander seeds (a must)

1½ Tbsp (22.5 mL) tomato paste

½ cauliflower (florets only), lightly steamed

½ cup (125 mL) chopped green olives

12 fresh basil leaves, roughly chopped

6 sundried tomatoes, halved and roughly chopped

4 canned artichoke hearts, chopped

3 Tbsp (45 mL) canned or frozen corn (thawed) (optional)

1 tsp (5 mL) sea salt

¼ cup (60 mL) agave or maple syrup

¼ cup (60 mL) apple cider vinegar

1. Heat the oil in a large nonstick saucepan set over medium heat.

2. Toss in the eggplant and onion, and sauté until they are slightly colored.

3. Add the celery and cook for 1 minute, tossing the ingredients around. Add a little extra olive oil if the pan is dry.

4. Add the peppers and continue to cook, stirring.

5. Add the carrot, garlic, chili and coriander seeds, and cook over low heat for a few minutes.

6. Stir in the remaining ingredients. Lower the heat to minimum, cover and cook gently for approximately 30 minutes, or until the vegetables have softened. Keep an eye on the mixture and stir gently from time to time.

7. Remove from the heat and allow to cool. Transfer the mixture to a seal-tight jar and add enough olive oil to cover completely, then refrigerate. It will keep in the fridge for several weeks.

NOTE: **You will need a sterilized jar with a capacity of approximately 4 cups (1 L)—I use a Le Parfait lever-seal jar.**

MOUTHWATERING VEGAN

PASTIZZI MAKES ABOUT 16 PASTRIES

PASTIZZI are a traditional Maltese savory snack made by filling puff pastry with either ricotta cheese ("cheesecakes"—quite different from the sweet dessert of that name) or a spicy pea filling ("peacakes"). There are pastizzerias all over Malta selling these popular pastries. So I decided to take on the challenge and produce veganized versions of both types of *pastizzi*—a tall order, given their hallowed reputation within these shores, but the results are spectacular! For best results, soak the split peas overnight.

SAVORY CHEESECAKE FILLING

1 12.3-oz (349-g) package firm silken tofu, drained

2 Tbsp (30 mL) French onion–flavored vegan cream cheese

1 cup (250 mL) grated vegan cheese that melts—use either Vegan Mozzarella (see page 253), Mild Cheddar "Cheese" (see page 254) or purchased

2 Tbsp (30 mL) teriyaki sauce (see page 127 or use purchased)

1 Tbsp (15 mL) finely chopped fresh parsley

2 tsp (10 mL) unbleached all-purpose flour

1 tsp (5 mL) Nutty Parmesan (see page 262 or use purchased)

PEACAKE FILLING

1 cup (250 mL) green split peas

baking soda, for sprinkling

2 large onions

1½ tsp (7.5 mL) curry powder (hot, if you like)

1 tsp (5 mL) fine garlic granules

1 tsp (5 mL) pumpkin pie spice

½ tsp (2 mL) turmeric

1 tsp (5 mL) vegetable stock granules or powder

salt to taste

2 slices vegan bacon, diced (optional)

olive oil

1 tsp (5 mL) tomato paste

1 Tbsp (15 mL) soy sauce

¼ cup (60 mL) water

vegan margarine, melted, for brushing

TO ASSEMBLE

8 oz (250 g) vegan puff pastry

SAVORY CHEESECAKE FILLING

1. Place the silken tofu in a large bowl and crumble it with your hands.

2. Add the cream cheese and mix with a spoon or fork.

3. Add the remaining ingredients and mix roughly with a fork. Set the mixture aside in the fridge for a few minutes to allow it to settle.

PEACAKE FILLING

1. Soak the split peas overnight in plenty of water. (Try not to skip this step, or else the peas will not be as tender.)

2. Drain the split peas and rinse them thoroughly. Sprinkle with baking soda, then rinse well again.

3. Place the split peas in a large saucepan, cover with water, bring to a boil and simmer until very soft, at least 1 hour—they should be the consistency of thick mashed potatoes.

4. When the peas are nearly done cooking, place the onions in a food processor and process until very finely chopped.

5. Transfer the onions to a large bowl and stir in the curry powder, garlic granules, pumpkin pie spice, turmeric, vegetable stock, salt and bacon (if using).

6. Heat the olive oil in a large, deep, nonstick pan and fry the onion mixture for about 10 minutes, stirring every few minutes so it won't burn.

7. Stir in the tomato paste and soy sauce, lower the heat and enjoy the aroma.

8. Once the peas have softened, drain them well so that no water remains and add to the onion mixture.

9. Mix well, add the water and cook for a further 15 minutes over low heat, stirring frequently to ensure it doesn't stick. Remove from the heat and cool.

NOTE: **This recipe makes enough filling for 2 batches, so you can freeze half for another time.**

(continued next page)

TO ASSEMBLE

1. Preheat the oven to 400°F (200°C). Oil a nonstick baking sheet.

2. Roll out your puff pastry on a well-floured kitchen surface. Cut out circles about 5 inches (12 cm) in diameter, using a knife to cut around a small bowl or, if you're steady-handed, cut freehand.

3. Place 1 heaped tsp (about 7 mL) of the tofu or peacake filling in the center of each pastry circle. Bring together the outer edges of the dough by lifting them up, then press the edges together to seal in the shape of a large shell.

4. For the peacake version only, pierce a slit in each of the pastizzi, and brush some melted margarine overtop.

5. Place the pastizzi on the prepared baking tray. Bake for about 30 minutes, until golden, and serve hot, with a cup of tea.

NOTE: I find that puff pastry is too time-consuming to make from scratch, and it's hard to beat a good-quality ready-made puff pastry (see page xxii).

ZESTY CAULIFLOWER
with Garlic & Basil SERVES 4

SIMPLE, HEALTHY AND DELICIOUS, this side dish—inspired by my mother's cauliflower drizzled with oil and lemon—can be thrown together in just a few minutes. It's an excellent way to eat your veggies in the winter, when you're not in the mood for a cold salad. To turn it into a main course, stir in a can of cannellini beans, or accompany with hummus (see the recipe on page 25) and a whole wheat baguette.

1 medium cauliflower (as white and tight as they come), cut into medium-sized florets

2–3 cloves garlic, very finely chopped

½ cup (125 mL) fresh basil, cilantro or flat-leaf parsley, roughly chopped

zest and juice of 1 lemon

salt and pepper to taste

drizzle of extra virgin olive oil

1. Steam the cauliflower for about 5 minutes in a vegetable steamer or in a saucepan with a little water, being careful not to overcook.

2. While the cauliflower is still warm, transfer it to a serving bowl. Add the remaining ingredients, toss gently and serve.

SOUPS & SALADS

GINGER & VEGGIE BROTH

SERVES 4

THIS REALLY SHOULD BE CALLED THE "HEALER'S BROTH," as its effects on a cold are nothing short of miraculous; the ginger makes it very decongesting, and the garlic and veggies yield many beneficial nutrients. But that name might not make it sound tempting enough, because it's just so delicious. An added bonus—it's extra simple to make.

---

3 Tbsp (45 mL) olive or canola oil

1 large onion, finely chopped

1 large carrot, diced

1 large zucchini, diced

3 garlic scapes, finely chopped (or 4 cloves garlic, chopped)

3 cloves garlic, chopped (yes, in addition to the above)

1 3-inch (8-cm) piece fresh ginger, finely diced (not grated, as you need the texture)

½ tsp (2 mL) ground coriander

1 15-oz (425-mL) can brown lentils, drained

salt to taste

1½ tsp (7.5 mL) vegetable stock granules or powder

4 cups (1 L) water

1½ Tbsp (22.5 mL) soy sauce

1. Heat the oil in a medium nonstick saucepan set over medium heat. Sauté the onion and carrot for a minute or so, stirring.

2. Add the zucchini, garlic scapes and cloves, ginger and coriander, and continue to cook, stirring, for another minute.

3. Now add the remaining ingredients, cover and simmer for about 30 minutes, or until the carrot is soft. Serve with crunchy garlic bread (see page 34).

GREEK "CHICKEN" & LEMON SOUP SERVES 4

SINCE I BECAME VEGETARIAN, I've often thought of how much I miss my mum's Greek Chicken Soup, and I dreamed of creating a vegan version. The traditional recipe, made with chicken, egg and lemon, is used by Greeks as a convalescing soup. This version will make you feel just as cozy and comforted, whether you're under the weather, or on top of it. Sprinkle with cinnamon and serve with a crunchy whole-grain baguette.

---

2 Tbsp (30 mL) olive oil

1 large white onion, cut in half lengthwise

1 medium carrot, cut in half

1 stalk celery, cut into thirds

1 clove garlic

4 cups (1 L) water

1 cup (250 mL) vegan chicken-flavored stock (see page xxi)

2 Tbsp (30 mL) short-grain rice (brown is preferable)

1 tsp (5 mL) vegan margarine

1 tsp (5 mL) nutritional yeast

¼ tsp (1 mL) turmeric

1 cup (250 mL) nondairy milk (see page 249 or use purchased)

4 Tbsp (60 mL) coconut milk

juice of 1 lemon

ground cinnamon, for sprinkling

1. Heat the olive oil in a nonstick soup pot set over low heat. Sauté the onion, carrot, celery and garlic clove for a few minutes, stirring.

2. Add the water, stock, rice, margarine, nutritional yeast and turmeric. Cover and bring to a boil. Reduce the heat and simmer for about 40 minutes, until the rice is fully cooked.

3. In a separate container, combine the milk, coconut milk and lemon juice. Using a handheld immersion blender, blend until smooth and creamy. Without this step, the soup will curdle when you add the milk and lemon mixture to the pot.

4. Using a fork or slotted spoon, remove the veggies from the soup and discard, leaving the rice in the broth.

5. Turn up the heat and slowly pour in the milk and lemon mixture. Heat for a few minutes, bringing it almost to a boil.

6. Taste for seasoning, then serve in soup bowls, sprinkled with cinnamon (a must, unless you don't like cinnamon—it truly makes the dish). Enjoy!

CARROT & APRICOT SOUP

SERVES 4

CARROTS AND APRICOTS COMBINE in a healing, rejuvenating, delicious soup that's loaded with beta-carotene. These ingredients might sound like they would be better served in a large glass with ice, but taste before you judge.

10 dried apricots

2 cups (500 mL) water

olive oil

3 large sweet carrots, chopped

1 large onion, chopped

4 cloves garlic, chopped

2½ cups (625 mL) vegetable stock

1½ cups (375 mL) soymilk

⅓ cup (80 mL) vegan cream (see page 249 or use purchased)

just over ¼ tsp (1 mL) ground nutmeg

salt to taste (don't omit this)

1. Combine the apricots and water in a small saucepan, cover and bring to a simmer. Reduce the heat and stew for about 40 minutes, until the liquid has reduced to ¼–½ cup (60–125 mL).

2. Heat a drizzle of oil in a medium nonstick saucepan and sauté the carrots and onion for a couple of minutes, stirring.

3. Add the garlic and stir for another minute. Add the stock, bring to a simmer, cover, reduce the heat and cook until the carrots soften—about 20 minutes.

4. Add the apricots with their cooking liquid and simmer over low heat for another 10 minutes.

5. Using a handheld immersion blender, process the soup until blended. Add the remaining ingredients (reserving a little cream to drizzle on top). Process again until smooth.

6. Return the soup to the saucepan and reheat gently over low heat.

7. Taste for salt—you will need a little more than usual to counteract the sweetness of the apricots.

8. Serve hot, drizzled with cream, and enjoy.

EASY SPINACH, LIME & GINGER SOUP SERVES 4

THIS SOUP IS INSPIRED BY MY GOOD FRIEND DAVE, who makes great food. It is full of nutrients and vitamins, and is so very warming and comforting on a cold winter's day. The spinach, garlic and ginger make it a great immune booster, too—and, best of all, it's so easy to make. It tastes best with fresh spinach, but you can use frozen, too.

2 Tbsp (30 mL) olive oil

1 medium onion, finely chopped

1½ tsp (7.5 mL) minced fresh ginger

3 garlic scapes or 2 cloves garlic, finely chopped

⅔ lb (350 g) frozen spinach, thawed, or 1 lb (500 g) fresh spinach

4 cups (1 L) water or vegetable stock

juice of 1 lime (or more to taste)

¼ tsp (1 mL) ground nutmeg

a pinch of ground cardamom

salt and freshly ground black pepper to taste

1. Heat the oil in a soup pot set over medium heat. Sauté the onion and ginger for a minute or so, add the garlic scapes or cloves and sauté for another minute.

2. Add the spinach (if you're using fresh, sauté until it has wilted) and cook, stirring, for 1 minute.

3. Add the water or stock, cover and bring to a boil. Reduce the heat and simmer for 20–30 minutes.

4. Remove from the heat and allow the soup to cool slightly, then transfer to your food processor (or blend using a handheld immersion blender).

5. Add the lime juice, nutmeg, cardamom, salt and pepper. Process for 1 minute, until completely smooth.

6. Transfer the soup back to the pot and reheat gently. Serve hot.

SWEET POTATO, LEEK & GINGER SOUP SERVES 4

I LOVE SWEET POTATOES in just about every size, shape and form. They are so delicious, even gently fried and served with a little garlic salt. Here, I have used them in a creamy, sweet soup, balanced by the mild onionlike flavor of leeks and the spiciness of ginger. This brought big smiles to my family's faces—it will do the same to yours.

extra virgin olive oil

2 medium sweet potatoes, peeled and cubed

2 medium leeks, chopped

1 2-inch (5-cm) piece fresh ginger, peeled and chopped

2 cloves garlic, finely chopped

3 cups (750 mL) mushroom stock

¾ cup (185 mL) coconut milk

salt and freshly ground black pepper to taste

vegan cream (see page 249 or use purchased), for topping

1. Heat a drizzle of olive oil in a large nonstick saucepan set over medium heat.

2. Sauté the sweet potatoes, leeks and ginger for a few minutes, stirring often.

3. Add the chopped garlic and continue to cook, stirring, for a minute or so.

4. Add the mushroom stock, cover and bring to a boil. Reduce the heat to medium–low and simmer for 30 minutes.

5. Once the veggies are soft, add the coconut milk and salt and pepper. Remove from the heat and allow to cool for a few minutes.

6. Transfer the soup to a blender (or use a handheld immersion blender) and blend until smooth and creamy.

7. Pour into bowls, then carefully pour some cream over the back of a teaspoon to top each serving. (This will keep the cream separate from the soup.)

MUSHROOM & SHERRY SOUP

SERVES 4

SOME YEARS BACK, a good friend made the most delectable cream of mushroom soup I had ever tasted. He claimed the recipe had been passed down from his grandmother— our friend was around 60 then, so you do the math. I kept the main ingredients in my mind and experimented with the rest to create a vegan version that easily rivalled the original. Top this comforting, delicious soup with garlicky croutons for that certain *je ne sais quoi*.

SOUP

2 Tbsp (30 mL) vegan margarine

2 Tbsp (30 mL) olive oil

2 medium onions, chopped

6 cloves garlic, chopped

1 lb (500 g) mushrooms (ideally porcini or shiitake, tough stems removed), finely chopped

½ tsp (2 mL) caraway seeds

4 cups (1 L) vegetable stock

2 cups (500 mL) nondairy milk (see page 249 or use purchased)

4 Tbsp (60 mL) sherry

1 tsp (5 mL) freshly ground black pepper

salt to taste

2 tsp (10 mL) teriyaki sauce (see page 127 or use purchased)

NEW LIFE CROUTONS

4 slices whole-grain bread

1 cup (250 mL) crushed walnuts

1 carrot, grated

2 spring or green onions, finely chopped

2 tsp (10 mL) garlic salt

SOUP

1. In a large nonstick saucepan set over low heat, melt together the margarine and oil. Add the onions and sauté until golden (don't overbrown them).

2. Add the garlic and sauté gently for a further minute.

3. Stir in the mushrooms and cook until they become limp, about 10 minutes.

4. Add the caraway seeds, stir and cook for a minute or so, then add 1 cup (250 mL) of the vegetable stock. Cover and leave to simmer for 10 minutes over low heat.

5. Add the rest of the stock and the milk, sherry, pepper and salt, and continue to simmer over low heat for 15–20 minutes.

6. Check that the mushrooms are tender, then lower the heat to minimum. Uncover, stir in the teriyaki sauce, then leave the soup to cool.

7. Taste for seasoning and add more salt if needed, then decant the soup into your blender and blend until very smooth.

8. Transfer the soup back to the saucepan and reheat it gently—don't let it boil. Serve hot. If you like it "hot" hot, grind on some more pepper!

CROUTONS

1. Toast the bread, crumble it into small pieces and combine with the remaining ingredients in a small bowl.

2. Garnish each bowl of soup with a sprinkling of New Life Croutons.

CREAM OF PORCINI MUSHROOM & CILANTRO SOUP SERVES 4

SIMPLY PUT, THIS SOUP ROCKS! It's very easy to make, and because it is so flavorful and rich, it can be served as an elegant starter for a dinner party or festive occasion, or as a comforting main meal with bread on a winter's day.

olive oil

2 medium leeks, roughly chopped

2 large porcini mushrooms, chopped

2 cloves garlic, finely chopped

1½ cups (375 mL) vegetable stock

3 cups (750 mL) water

1½ cups (375 mL) vegan cream (see page 249 or use purchased)

a handful of fresh cilantro, chopped

sea salt to taste

1. Heat a drizzle of oil in a soup pot set over medium heat. Sauté the leeks for a few moments, then stir in the mushrooms and garlic.

2. Lower the heat, cover and allow the veggies to cook for a couple of minutes. Stir again.

3. Add the vegetable stock and water, cover and simmer for 20 minutes or so, until the leeks are soft.

4. Add the cream, cilantro and salt, and blend until smooth using a handheld immersion blender. If it's too thick, blend in a little more water, then serve.

CREAMY COCONUT BROCCOLI SOUP SERVES 4

I HAVE A COMPLETE FIXATION ON COCONUT. Its flavor and creaminess are sublime, and there's constant news about its amazing health benefits. This easy, super-fast recipe has a double boost of coconut—both oil and milk—to take it into the yummy zone. When I first made this, my daughter—who was four years old and thought she didn't like broccoli—pronounced it her favorite soup ever.

3 Tbsp (45 mL) unsweetened coconut oil

1 large onion, roughly chopped

1 large head broccoli, cut into florets

3 cloves garlic, roughly chopped

¾ cup (185 mL) vegetable stock

3 cups (750 mL) coconut milk (a rich, creamy kind—not reduced-fat)

salt to taste

1½ Tbsp (22.5 mL) chopped fresh cilantro

3 cups (750 mL) water

lime wedges, for garnish

1. Heat the coconut oil in a soup pot set over medium heat.

2. Add the onion and broccoli and sauté over medium–low heat for 10 minutes, stirring. Add the garlic and continue stirring for another minute.

3. Next, add the stock and cover. Allow to simmer for 15–20 minutes.

4. Stir in the coconut milk, cover and cook for another 10 minutes.

5. Remove from heat and allow to cool for a few minutes, then add the salt and cilantro.

6. Blend until smooth using a handheld immersion blender. The soup will be very thick. Add the water and blend again.

7. Transfer the soup back to the pot and reheat gently over low heat. Serve immediately, with lime wedges on the side for squeezing overtop.

CREAM OF LEEK, ZUCCHINI & PARSLEY SOUP SERVES 4

THIS SOUP COULDN'T BE EASIER TO MAKE, with only a handful of simple, fresh ingredients. It's a tasty, healthy showcase for the delicate flavors of leeks and zucchini, perked up by the fresh parsley. Rosemary Garlic Bread (see the recipe on page 34) is the perfect accompaniment.

4 Tbsp (60 mL) olive oil

4 leeks, chopped

4 medium zucchini, chopped

4 cups (1 L) water, vegetable stock or a combination

salt and freshly ground black pepper to taste

2 or 3 sprigs fresh parsley, chopped

½ cup (125 mL) vegan cream (see page 249 or use purchased)

1. Heat the oil in a soup pot set over medium heat, and sauté the leeks and zucchini until they're a little transparent.

2. Add the water and/or stock and the salt and pepper. Bring to a boil, then cover and simmer for 20 minutes over low heat.

3. Stir in the finely chopped parsley and cook, covered, for another 15 minutes. When the veggies are soft, remove the pot from the heat and stir in the cream.

4. Using a handheld immersion blender, blend the soup until smooth. Serve hot, with garlic bread.

HOME SWEET HOME SOUP

SERVES 4

THIS IS JUST WHAT YOU WANT TO COME HOME TO on a cold winter's day—hearty, tasty and mouthwatering. Packed with nutrients and proteins, this filling dish is a meal in itself—something between a soup and a stew, with a sublime texture and aroma. Round it off perfectly with a hot baguette, and get warm!

olive oil

2 leeks, chopped

1 potato, chopped

1 slice smoked vegan bacon, chopped (optional)

1 14-oz (398-mL) can chopped tomatoes

2 Tbsp (30 mL) tomato paste

½ cup (125 mL) pearl barley, rinsed thoroughly

1 tsp (5 mL) vegetable stock granules

1 cup (250 mL) fresh or frozen fava beans or shelled edamame beans

½ cup (125 mL) red lentils

1 Tbsp (15 mL) nutritional yeast (optional)

salt to taste

6 cups (1.5 L) water, plus extra as needed

1. Heat a drizzle of oil in a medium saucepan set over medium heat. Sauté the leeks and potato for a couple of minutes.

2. Add the bacon (if using), followed by the tomatoes and tomato paste, and cook, stirring, for another couple of minutes.

3. Add the barley and the remaining ingredients except the water and cook for a few more minutes, stirring constantly.

4. Add 1 cup (250 mL) of the water, cover and simmer for about 1 hour, adding the remaining water a cup at a time, every 10 minutes or so. Adjust the consistency if desired by adding more water—legumes absorb a lot of liquid as they cook.

5. The soup is ready once the barley has softened and the lentils are tender. Serve hot with crunchy bread of your choice.

BEST-EVER WINTER SOUP SERVES 4

THIS IS ONE OF THE BEST SOUPS EVER, and a meal in itself with hot, crunchy garlic bread. The combination of hearty chickpeas, earthy spinach and Indian spices brings delight, warmth, comfort and satisfaction on a chilly day. If that isn't enough, it's simple to make and packed with protein, iron, calcium and vitamin C.

olive oil

2 large spring or green onions, chopped

2 tsp (10 mL) garam masala

4 tsp (20 mL) curry powder (hot, if you like)

1 tsp (5 mL) ground ginger

2 14-oz (398-mL) cans chickpeas, drained and rinsed

1 28-oz (796-mL) can diced tomatoes with juice

2 tsp (10 mL) vegan brown sugar

4 Tbsp (60 mL) soy sauce

1 Tbsp (15 mL) vegetable stock granules or powder

2 tsp (10 mL) fine garlic granules or powder

2 tsp (10 mL) Marmite (or other vegan yeast extract—see page xx)

6 cups (1.5 L) water

12 oz (375 g) frozen spinach, thawed

2 tsp (10 mL) chopped fresh cilantro

1. Heat a drizzle of oil in a medium soup pot set over medium–low heat, and sauté the onions until tender, stirring frequently.

2. Add all the spices, stir and indulge in the emanating aroma for a minute or so.

3. Add the chickpeas and cook, stirring, for another couple of minutes.

4. Add the canned tomatoes, bring to a simmer, cover, reduce the heat and cook for 10 minutes.

5. Uncover, and stir in the remaining ingredients except the cilantro. Lower the heat and simmer for another 20 minutes or so, until the soup is a nice, thick consistency.

6. Ladle into bowls, sprinkle the cilantro on top and serve immediately.

CHERRY TOMATO SOUP SERVES 4

CHERRY TOMATOES HAVE A SWEET, almost grapelike flavor that adds a twist to the classic tomato soup. For a heavenly light meal, accompany with Rosemary Garlic Bread (see the recipe on page 34).

8 Tbsp (120 mL) extra virgin olive oil

about 40 cherry tomatoes, halved

2 leeks, chopped

2 Tbsp (30 mL) tomato paste

6 cloves garlic, chopped

3 cups (750 mL) vegetable stock

3 cups (750 mL) water

2 Tbsp (30 mL) vegan margarine

1 tsp (5 mL) raw or turbinado sugar

salt to taste

1. Heat the olive oil in a nonstick soup pot set over medium heat, and fry the cherry tomatoes for a few minutes, until bruised.

2. Add the chopped leeks and cook, stirring. When the leeks are slightly golden in color, add the tomato paste and continue to stir for a few minutes, until the oil turns slightly orange.

3. Add the garlic, lower the heat and stir for about 1 minute.

4. Add the remaining ingredients and simmer for 30 minutes.

5. Remove the soup from the heat, and leave to cool for 30 minutes.

6. Using a handheld immersion blender, blend the soup until smooth and thick. If you'd like a creamier soup, blend in 2 Tbsp (30 mL) of vegan cream (see page 249 or use purchased).

7. Return the soup to the pot and reheat gently, then serve.

MIXED LETTUCE SALAD
with Strawberries, Pear & Basil SERVES 4

WITH ITS COMBINATION OF GREENS, antioxidant-rich berries, high-protein seeds and ginger—which is naturally anti-inflammatory—this salad is a wealth of health in a bowl. The contrasting colors of red and green and complementary textures and flavors make this a feast for all the senses.

SALAD

a handful of mixed lettuce, roughly chopped

8 strawberries, quartered

1 juicy pear, cored and cubed

1 carrot, julienned

½ cup (125 mL) fresh basil, roughly chopped

1 clove garlic, finely chopped

1 Tbsp (15 mL) grated fresh ginger

1 Tbsp (15 mL) pumpkin seeds

1 Tbsp (15 mL) sunflower seeds

DRESSING

5 Tbsp (75 mL) balsamic vinegar

5 Tbsp (75 mL) olive oil

1 Tbsp (15 mL) maple syrup

sea salt to taste

SALAD

1. Mix the lettuce, strawberries, pear, carrot, basil and garlic in a large bowl.

2. Sprinkle the grated ginger on top—it looks fabulous that way, and smells heavenly too.

3. Sprinkle on the seeds.

DRESSING

1. Whisk together the dressing ingredients in a small bowl, and drizzle over the salad.

CHERRY TOMATO, CHICKPEA & ORANGE PEPPER SALAD SERVES 4

RICH IN IRON AND VITAMINS A AND C, this salad is both delicious and filling. It's a wonderful warm-weather dish, and can be eaten as a main course with fresh Italian ciabatta dipped in a little olive oil and lemon, or as an accompaniment to a quiche or any other light meal.

DRESSING

juice of 1 large lemon

½ cup (125 mL) extra virgin olive oil

½ tsp (2 mL) vegan sugar

salt and freshly ground black pepper to taste

SALAD

20 cherry tomatoes, halved

1½ cups (375 mL) cooked chickpeas

1 medium red onion, finely chopped

4 cloves garlic, finely chopped

a handful of fresh flat-leaf parsley, finely chopped

1 small orange bell pepper, sliced thinly in strips, then cut twice crossways

12 fresh basil leaves, finely chopped

DRESSING

1. Place the ingredients in a clean jar, close the lid tightly and shake until thick and smooth.

SALAD

1. Toss all the ingredients together in a bowl.

2. Drizzle on as much dressing as you like, toss again and serve.

STUFFED ICEBERG PARCELS SERVES 4

MY MOTHER—OF GREEK ORIGIN—used to make vine leaves stuffed with rice and aromatic spices, but only a few times a year, as she claimed it was such hard work. This version using lettuce leaves (and an extra kick of spice) is much easier and quicker to make, but just as impressive looking and delicious. Served with a glass of fresh fruit juice, it makes a nutritious, light lunch.

---

olive or sunflower oil

2 cups (500 mL) cooked short-grain brown or white rice (see page xvi)

2 tsp (10 mL) curry powder

a pinch of ground cardamom

1 tsp (5 mL) paprika

20 walnuts, chopped roughly

2 small carrots, finely diced or grated

1 small red onion or 3–4 small green onions, finely chopped

8 leaves each fresh mint and basil, finely chopped

4 Tbsp (60 mL) sultana raisins

about 10 chopped Greek or Spanish black olives

dash of fresh lemon juice (optional)

a pinch of salt

4 large iceberg lettuce leaves, washed and dried well

1. Heat a drizzle of oil in a nonstick pan set over medium heat. Fry the cooked rice and spices for a couple of minutes, then remove from the heat and allow to cool completely.

2. Add the rest of the ingredients except the lettuce and blend well using a fork.

3. Heap 2–3 large spoonfuls of filling in the center of each lettuce leaf and roll up. Use a couple of toothpicks to keep it together. Serve immediately.

MIDDLE EASTERN SALAD

SERVES 4 AS AN APPETIZER OR 2 AS A MAIN COURSE

ZESTY, SATISFYING AND NUTRIENT-PACKED, this combination of creamy beans, crunchy vegetables and fragrant herbs is a perfect main-course salad, served with a hot, crunchy whole-grain baguette. It would also be a fantastic accompaniment to virtually any meal. The sublime range of Middle Eastern flavors is showcased here—sweetness, a touch of spice and lots of zing!

DRESSING

1 tsp (5 mL) dried mint

1 tsp (5 mL) curry powder

salt (it will need it) and freshly ground black pepper to taste

1 Tbsp (15 mL) agave or maple syrup

juice of 2 lemons

4 Tbsp (60 mL) extra virgin olive oil

SALAD

2 14-oz (398-mL) cans cannellini beans, drained and rinsed

12 cherry tomatoes, diced

1 small red bell pepper, diced

1 medium English cucumber (unpeeled), finely diced

2 green onions, finely chopped

3 large cloves garlic, finely chopped

¾ cup (185 mL) arugula or radicchio

a handful of bean sprouts (optional)

zest of 1 lemon or other citrus fruit

8 fresh basil leaves, chopped

a handful of fresh flat-leaf parsley, finely chopped

DRESSING

1. Combine all the dressing ingredients in a tight-lidded jar and shake well.

SALAD

1. Combine all the salad ingredients in a bowl.

2. Drizzle on the dressing, toss well and serve.

NOTE: **The trick with this salad is to chop each ingredient very finely.**

MONSOON SALAD SERVES 4

HERE IS THE MOST MAGNIFICENT Indian-style pasta salad imaginable. Full of color, vitality and a diverse range of ingredients—including succulent mangoes, crunchy pecans and savory olives—it possesses a luscious texture and sensual aroma. Ideal for a spring or summer lunch or picnic dish.

10 oz (300 g) dry fusilli pasta

1½ cups (375 mL) Mayo from the Heavens (see page 250 or use purchased)

1½ cups (375 mL) plain nondairy yogurt

6 Tbsp (90 mL) olive oil

4 Tbsp (60 mL) maple syrup

2 Tbsp (30 mL) tomato paste

4 tsp (20 mL) fine garlic granules

2 tsp (10 mL) toasted sesame seeds, plus extra for garnish

2 tsp (10 mL) curry powder

1 tsp (5 mL) turmeric

2 fresh mangoes, finely diced

2 cups (500 mL) canned or frozen corn (thawed)

2 green onions, finely chopped

½ small red bell pepper, finely diced

½ cup (125 mL) pecans, roughly chopped, plus extra for garnish

16 Kalamata olives, chopped

salt and freshly ground black pepper to taste

a few drops of lemon juice

1. Cook the pasta according to the package directions, drain and allow to cool completely.

2. In a large bowl, combine the remaining ingredients, adding them in the order listed, starting with the wet ingredients, then the powdered ones, followed by the rest, stirring between each addition. Gently stir in the cooked pasta.

3. Taste for seasoning and add more salt if needed. Sprinkle with extra pecans and sesame seeds for garnish. Serve immediately at room temperature, or refrigerate and serve cold.

RAINBOW RICE SALAD SERVES 4

DELICIOUS, COLORFUL, GREAT FOR BEACH TRIPS AND PICNICS, as a side dish for vegan barbecues or for a light lunch—you name it. The diverse and contrasting flavors are there to be enjoyed. Once you chop everything, the rest is fast and easy . . . as is eating it.

1 cup (250 mL) cooked long-grain white rice

2 green onions, finely chopped

¾ cup (185 mL) diced mixed red and green bell peppers

1 cup (250 mL) canned or frozen corn (thawed)

½ cup (125 mL) chopped walnuts or pecans

1 medium zucchini, finely diced

¼ cup (60 mL) chopped fresh parsley

¼ cup (60 mL) chopped fresh mint

6 olives, pitted and diced

½ cup (125 mL) vegan cheese, cut into small cubes—use either Vegan Mozzarella (see page 253), Mild Cheddar "Cheese" (see page 254) or purchased

1 apple, diced

¼ cup (60 mL) sultana raisins

2 Tbsp (30 mL) chopped fresh basil

2 Tbsp (30 mL) olive oil

zest of ½ lemon

juice of 1 lemon

1½ tsp (7.5 mL) curry powder

salt and pepper to taste

1. Place the cooked rice in a medium bowl and add the remaining ingredients.

2. Stir well and serve immediately. Refrigerate any leftovers for up to 2 days.

WILD RICE SALAD SERVES 4

THIS SALAD HAS FAR TOO MANY BENEFITS TO MENTION HERE. Suffice it to say, the ingredients are highly nutritious, the taste is sublime and it won't be an effort to indulge. Enjoy!

SALAD

1 cup (250 mL) mixed red and black wild rice

3 cups (750 mL) water

1 medium spring or green onion, finely chopped

a large handful of fresh cilantro, finely chopped

½ small red bell pepper, finely chopped

12 mushrooms, finely chopped and gently fried in unsweetened coconut oil

1 avocado, peeled, pitted and finely chopped

2 tsp (10 mL) raw sesame seeds

20 walnut halves, chopped

5 raw almonds, chopped

1 Tbsp (15 mL) grated fresh ginger

zest of 1 lime

DRESSING

juice of 1 lime

1 tsp (5 mL) unsweetened coconut oil

1 Tbsp (15 mL) olive or flaxseed oil

¼ tsp (1 mL) turmeric

2½ tsp (12.5 mL) rice vinegar

¼ cup (60 mL) pomegranate juice

2 Tbsp (30 mL) teriyaki sauce (see page 127 or use purchased)

sea salt to taste

SALAD

1. Combine the rice and water in a saucepan and bring to a boil. Cover, reduce the heat and simmer until the rice is cooked, about 1 hour. Drain, rinse, and set aside until cooled.

2. Combine the cooled rice with the remaining salad ingredients in a serving bowl.

3. Drizzle on the dressing. You may not wish to use it all, so pour with caution and taste for salt and sweetness.

4. Serve immediately or store in the fridge for up to 2 days.

DRESSING

1. Place the dressing ingredients in a jar with a tight-fitting lid and shake well to combine.

PASTA, PIZZA & BURGERS

FIVE PERFECT PESTO VARIATIONS EACH RECIPE YIELDS 4 GENEROUS SERVINGS

EVERYBODY LOVES PESTO—it's healthy, addictive and can be tossed together in a food processor in minutes while the pasta is cooking, for the ultimate convenient meal. I can't seem to stop experimenting with different versions, so here are five pestos, ranging from classic to unique, all sure to delight your palate. Most will keep for over a week in the fridge, so long as you seal the top with olive oil.

ALMOND & BASIL PESTO

½ cup (125 mL) blanched whole almonds

3 cloves garlic

3 cups (750 mL) loosely packed fresh basil leaves

½ cup (125 mL) extra virgin olive oil

1 slice vegan cheese—use either Vegan Mozzarella (see page 253), Mild Cheddar "Cheese" (see page 254) or purchased

salt and freshly ground black pepper to taste

PESTO INFERNO

¾ cup (185 mL) raw peanuts

2 large cloves garlic

2 cups (500 mL) fresh flat-leaf parsley, tough stems removed

6 sundried tomato halves, roughly chopped

½ cup (125 mL) extra virgin olive oil

1 Tbsp (15 mL) nutritional yeast

½ cup (125 mL) grated vegan cheese—use either Vegan Mozzarella (see page 253), Mild Cheddar "Cheese" (see page 254) or purchased

just under ¼ cup (60 mL) cold water

salt to taste

½ red bell pepper, diced and sautéed in olive oil for a few minutes with 1 finely chopped red chili

freshly ground black pepper to taste

extra diced red bell pepper, for garnish

CREAMY PARSLEY, BASIL & PECAN PESTO

4 cloves garlic

¾ cup (185 mL) pecans

5 Tbsp (75 mL) chopped fresh flat-leaf parsley

6 Tbsp (90 mL) chopped fresh basil leaves

6 Tbsp (90 mL) extra virgin olive oil

½ cup (125 mL) vegan cheese—use either Vegan Mozzarella (see page 253), Mild Cheddar "Cheese" (see page 254) or purchased

sea salt to taste

1 Tbsp (15 mL) water

¾ cup (185 mL) vegan cream (see page 249 or use purchased)

¼ red bell pepper, finely diced, for garnish

sprinkle of sweet paprika, for garnish

Nutty Parmesan (see page 262) or use purchased, for garnish (optional)

chopped fresh flat-leaf parsley, for garnish

(continued next page)

PARSLEY, BLACK OLIVE & WALNUT PESTO

12 walnuts, halved

3 large cloves garlic

about 2 cups (500 mL) fresh flat-leaf parsley, tough stems removed

8 salty black olives, pitted

2 Tbsp (30 mL) olive oil

2 Tbsp (30 mL) sunflower oil

a pinch of salt to taste

½ tsp (2 mL) freshly ground black pepper

¼ cup (60 mL) chopped or grated vegan cheese—use either Vegan Mozzarella (see page 253), Mild Cheddar "Cheese" (see page 254) or purchased (optional)

3–4 sundried tomatoes, chopped, for garnish (optional)

PEANUT, PARSLEY & CHILI PESTO

2 cloves garlic

¾ cup (185 mL) raw peanuts

1–2 red chilies, chopped

2 cups (500 mL) fresh flat-leaf parsley, tough stems removed

¼ cup (60 mL) olive oil

sea salt to taste

1 Tbsp (15 mL) Nutty Parmesan (see page 262 or use purchased)

1 Tbsp (15 mL) nutritional yeast

1 cup (250 mL) vegan cream (see page 249 or use purchased)

1. Cook the pasta of your choice (about 5 oz/150 g per person) according to package directions.

2. In a food processor, process the pesto ingredients in the order listed, starting with hard ingredients such as nuts and garlic, then adding herbs and greens, then oil and remaining ingredients. Scrape down the sides with a spatula and continue processing until you have a smooth paste.

3. Transfer the pesto to a large nonstick pan and heat over low for 1 minute. Toss in the cooked, drained pasta and stir well, until the pesto and pasta are heated through.

4. Garnish as desired and serve.

SPINACH, BASIL & ARUGULA

PESTO with Curried Vine Tomatoes SERVES 4

THIS COMBINATION OF PASTA TOSSED with a creamy, nutty green pesto and topped with sweet, scorched tomatoes is absolutely magical, and makes for a very special dinner. Indulge by serving with a glass of chilled white wine. But skip the side dishes—this pasta warrants your undivided attention.

---

1 cup (250 mL) hazelnuts, lightly toasted in a frying pan

½ cup (125 mL) raw cashews

4 cloves garlic

4 cups (1 L) packed fresh baby spinach

2 cups (500 mL) loosely packed fresh basil leaves

2 cups (500 mL) loosely packed arugula

½ cup (125 mL) extra virgin olive oil, plus extra for drizzling

2 tsp (10 mL) sea salt

2 Tbsp (30 mL) grated vegan cheese—use either Vegan Mozzarella (see page 253), Mild Cheddar "Cheese" (see page 254) or purchased

2 cups (500 mL) vegan cream (see page 249 or use purchased)

1 lb (500 g) dried spaghetti or other pasta

olive oil

about 24 small whole vine tomatoes

2 tsp (10 mL) coriander seeds

1 tsp (5 mL) curry powder

salt to taste

1 tsp (5 mL) freshly ground black pepper

1. Place the nuts and garlic in a food processor and process until small crumbs are formed.

2. Add the greens, and process until shredded into very small pieces.

3. Add the oil, salt and cheese and cream, and process until smooth.

4. Taste for salt, then set aside.

5. Meanwhile, get your pasta on the boil and cook according to package instructions.

6. Next, prepare the tomatoes: pour a little olive oil in a nonstick frying pan set over medium heat, and fry the tomatoes until they begin to brown.

7. Sprinkle on the coriander seeds, curry powder, salt and pepper, and allow the tomatoes to slightly scorch (no need to burn them). Set aside.

8. Transfer the pesto to a large nonstick pan and heat over low for 1 minute. Toss in the cooked, drained pasta and stir well.

9. Divide the pasta among 4 plates, gently spoon 6 tomatoes on top of each serving and enjoy!

SUNDRIED TOMATO, ARTICHOKE & HAZELNUT PEPPERED PESTO SERVES 4

THIS IS A SUBTLE, YET MOST MEMORABLE pesto featuring a unique combination of ingredients. Exquisite, succulent and aromatic, it's a true ensemble of tastes that plays a delicious culinary symphony.

1 lb (500 g) dried pasta of your choice

2 cloves garlic

½ cup (125 mL) toasted hazelnuts

½ cup (125 mL) fresh flat-leaf parsley, plus extra for garnish

4 marinated artichoke hearts

4 sundried tomatoes

4 Tbsp (60 mL) extra virgin olive oil

½ cup (125 mL) chopped or grated Vegan Mozzarella (see page 253) or other vegan cheese that melts

salt to taste

1 cup (250 mL) nondairy milk (see page 249 or use purchased)

chopped fresh parsley, for garnish

1 tsp (5 mL) crushed black peppercorns, for garnish

1. Put the pasta on to boil and cook according to package directions.

2. Meanwhile, place the garlic and nuts in the food processor and process until very finely chopped. Add the parsley and pulse again until finely chopped.

3. Add the artichoke hearts and sundried tomatoes and process again. Then add the oil, cheese and salt, and pulse until well blended.

4. When the pasta is cooked, drain it and rinse briefly with cold water. Transfer the pesto mixture to a saucepan with half the milk, and stir over low heat for 1 minute, or just until warmed.

5. Toss in the cooked pasta and stir in the remaining milk. Leave the saucepan over low heat until the pasta is heated through. Taste for seasoning and add more salt if needed.

6. Serve garnished with chopped fresh parsley and crushed black peppercorns.

BEST-EVER BOLOGNESE SERVES 4

BOLOGNESE SAUCE IS A FAVORITE IN OUR HOUSEHOLD, and over the years I have tweaked the recipe to perfection. Omnivores will not miss the meat, or likely even notice the lack of it. This merges the savory taste of classic Bolognese with a twist of sweetness, making for a very satisfying dish indeed. Serve it with the pasta of your choice.

1 medium potato, finely diced

extra virgin olive oil

1 medium onion, very finely chopped (you can do this in the food processor to save time)

2–3 cloves garlic, finely chopped

2 cups (500 mL) vegan ground meat substitute, crushed pecans, processed vegan burger or a combination

2 Tbsp (30 mL) tomato paste

½ tsp (2 mL) coriander seeds (optional)

½ tsp (2 mL) apple pie spice or allspice

½ tsp (2 mL) hot curry powder

1 14-oz (398-mL) can good-quality diced tomatoes

1 tsp (5 mL) agave, maple syrup or vegan brown sugar

1 tsp (5 mL) sea salt

1 tsp (5 mL) vegan margarine (optional)

1 Tbsp (15 mL) nutritional yeast

1 cup (250 mL) water

3 Tbsp (45 mL) amontillado or other medium-dry sherry (try not to omit this)

chopped fresh flat-leaf parsley, for garnish

1. Steam the diced potato in a saucepan or vegetable steamer until soft. Drain and set aside.

2. Heat a drizzle of oil in a large nonstick saucepan set over medium heat. Toss in the onion and garlic and stir, making sure they don't burn.

3. When the onion is translucent, add the ground meat substitute, and continue to cook, stirring, for another 5–10 minutes, so the flavors merge.

4. Add the tomato paste and spices, continuing to mix for a few more minutes.

5. Add the remaining ingredients except the water, sherry and parsley. Stir and allow to cook for a few more minutes, adding a little water and sherry at a time, until all of the liquid has been added.

6. Cover and simmer very gently over low heat for 20 minutes.

7. Taste for seasoning—your tongue should resonate with a wonderful balance of sweet and savory. If need be, add more agave or salt to reach that "note."

8. Garnish with fresh parsley.

NUTTY RAGÙ BOLOGNESE

SERVES 4

RAGÙ BOLOGNESE IS A FAVORITE OF MINE. Both the Italian *ragù* and the French *ragoût* derive from the verb *ragoûter*, which means "to revive the taste" or "to stimulate the appetite." The Italian version is native to Bologna and is traditionally made with ground beef, white wine, onions, tomatoes, various other vegetables—often including carrots and celery—and seasonings. For this vegan version, I substitute nuts for the meat, and then do my own take on the veggies and seasonings. The result is aromatic, delicious and filling.

---

extra virgin olive oil

1 carrot, finely chopped

1 red onion, finely chopped

3 cloves garlic, finely chopped

2 green onions, chopped

½ zucchini, finely chopped

½ cup (125 mL) small peas

1½ cups (375 mL) pecans, crushed

¼ cup (60 mL) pine nuts

2 Tbsp (30 mL) tomato paste

1 cup (250 mL) red wine

1 tsp (5 mL) each coriander seeds and fennel seeds

1 tsp (5 mL) curry powder

1 14-oz (398-mL) can diced tomatoes

a handful of fresh herbs (basil, rosemary and oregano), chopped

1 tsp (5 mL) vegan margarine

salt and freshly ground black pepper to taste

1 lb (500 g) dried spaghetti or other pasta

1 Tbsp (15 mL) chopped fresh parsley, for garnish

1. Heat a drizzle of olive oil in a large saucepan set over medium heat. Sauté all the vegetables together until they become slightly transparent.

2. Add the pecans and pine nuts and cook for a few minutes, stirring, until they take on some color.

3. Add the tomato paste and cook for a few minutes.

4. Add the wine and spices, and continue to cook for a few minutes, stirring.

5. Stir in the chopped tomatoes, followed by the remainder of the ingredients except the spaghetti and parsley.

6. Allow to simmer over low heat for 30 minutes, or until the carrot is soft—that will indicate that the ragù is ready. Add a little water if the sauce gets too dry.

7. Meanwhile, cook the pasta according to package directions. Drain and mix into the ragù sauce, then serve immediately, garnishing with some fresh parsley.

SPAGHETTI with Spinach & Mushrooms

SERVES 4

TASTY, HEARTY, FILLING AND, MOST OF ALL, simple and fast to make—for such little effort, the reward of this dish is so gratifying. If you have spaghetti, spinach (frozen will do the trick), garlic and a few mushrooms knocking around in your fridge, together with a couple of other basic things—then ready, steady, go! A glass of white wine makes a nice accompaniment.

1 lb (500 g) dried spaghetti

olive oil

8 cloves garlic, chopped

2 cups (500 mL) porcini or other mushrooms, chopped

10 oz (300 g) frozen spinach, thawed

2 Tbsp (30 mL) nutritional yeast

2 Tbsp (30 mL) vegan cream cheese

1 tsp (5 mL) dried oregano

4 Tbsp (60 mL) dry white wine

2 cups (500 mL) vegan cream (see page 249 or use purchased)

smoked paprika and freshly ground black pepper, for dusting

1. Cook the pasta according to package directions, until al dente. Drain and rinse in cold water.

2. While the pasta cooks, heat a drizzle of olive oil in a nonstick frying pan set over medium heat. Gently sauté the garlic for 1 minute, stirring to ensure it doesn't burn.

3. Add the mushrooms and lower the heat. Allow them to cook for a few minutes, until they release their juices.

4. Stir in the spinach and cook for 1 minute.

5. Add the yeast, cream cheese, oregano and wine. Cook for 10–15 minutes, uncovered, so that some of the liquid evaporates.

6. When the sauce has reduced, lower the heat to minimum and add the cream. Stir, and cook for a few more minutes, leaving the pan uncovered.

7. Add the cooked pasta to the sauce. Serve immediately, topped with a dusting of smoked paprika and pepper.

BAKED MACARONI MADNESS

SERVES 4 GENEROUSLY

THIS IS NO ORDINARY MACARONI, by any standard. Pasta bakes are a specialty of mine, but on this occasion I lost the plot in the kitchen, as I was determined to create the best-ever baked macaroni in the universe. The result—in a word, sublime! Serve with a simple salad of greens and herbs.

WHITE "CHEESE" SAUCE

1 cup (250 mL) vegan cream (see page 249 or use purchased)

½ cup (125 mL) water

2 Tbsp (30 mL) tapioca flour

2 Tbsp (30 mL) nutritional yeast

1 tsp (5 mL) sea salt

1 cup (250 mL) grated vegan cheese that melts—use either Vegan Mozzarella (see page 253), Mild Cheddar "Cheese" (see page 254) or purchased

a pinch of ground nutmeg

1 tsp (5 mL) garlic powder

PASTA

14 oz (400 g) dried short, ridged pasta, like rigatoni or tortiglioni

2 parsnips, finely diced

olive oil

1 small onion, finely chopped

3 cloves garlic, finely chopped

1 green chili, finely chopped

1 cup (250 mL) porcini or other mushrooms, chopped

2 cups (500 mL) vegan ground meat substitute, hydrated TVP (see page xviii) or crushed pecans

½ tsp (2 mL) coriander seeds

1 tsp (5 mL) curry powder

SAUCE

1. Place all the ingredients in the food processor and process until smooth.

2. Transfer the sauce to a small saucepan set over medium heat. Heat, stirring, until the sauce thickens nicely—it needs to be a medium-thick, pourable consistency, not a blob. Remove from the heat and set aside.

PASTA

1. Cook the pasta according to package directions. Drain it and rinse in cold water, then set aside in a large bowl.

2. Steam the parsnips in a vegetable steamer or saucepan until they're a little soft, then drain and set aside until cooled.

3. Heat a drizzle of olive oil in a large nonstick pan set over medium heat. Add the onion and sauté, stirring, until translucent.

4. Add the garlic, chili and mushrooms, continuing to stir.

5. Stir in the ground meat substitute, then the coriander seeds and curry powder, and continue cooking, stirring, for 1 minute.

6. Add the spinach and red pepper. Lower the heat and simmer for 10 minutes.

7. Add the tomato paste, olives (if using) and salt, and adjust the seasoning as necessary.

(continued next page)

⅔ lb (350 g) frozen spinach, thawed

½ cup (125 mL) finely chopped red bell pepper

3 Tbsp (45 mL) tomato paste

10 Greek black olives, pitted and chopped (optional)

salt to taste

vegan cheese, for topping—use either Vegan Mozzarella (see page 253), Mild Cheddar "Cheese" (see page 254) or purchased

paprika, for dusting

fresh thyme, for topping (optional)

Nutty Parmesan (see page 262 or use purchased), for serving (optional)

8. Preheat the oven to 400°F (200°C) and grease a deep casserole dish (at least 3 inches/8 cm deep).

9. Tip the cooked macaroni into the saucepan and give it a good toss, making sure everything has blended well.

10. Place half the macaroni mixture into the prepared dish. Pour all the white "cheese" sauce overtop, sprinkle on a handful of the cooked parsnips and top with cheese, dotting it around the dish.

11. Add the remaining macaroni and scatter the remaining parsnips on top.

12. Drizzle with olive oil and sprinkle with salt, paprika, and a little fresh thyme, if you like. Also, stand a few pieces of macaroni facing upward—they will burn slightly, but they will be crunchy and very yummy.

13. Bake for 40 minutes or until dark golden on top. Serve with Nutty Parmesan passed around at the table for topping, if you like.

CHEESY CAULIFLOWER PASTA BAKE SERVES 4

IT ALL STARTED WITH A SMALL CAULIFLOWER IN THE FRIDGE and me wondering, "Now, what can I do with you?" Soon it was transformed into this creamy, cheesy baked angel hair pasta dish, studded with cherry tomatoes and basil. The result is super-delicious, and a quickly prepared recipe the whole family will enjoy. Serve with a salad of your choice.

250 g (8 oz) dried angel hair pasta

1 small cauliflower, florets only

2 Tbsp (30 mL) vegan margarine, melted

2½ cups (625 mL) grated vegan cheese that melts—use either Vegan Mozzarella (see page 253), Mild Cheddar "Cheese" (see page 254) or purchased

olive oil, for drizzling

salt and pepper to taste

1½ cups (375 mL) vegan cream (see page 249 or use purchased)

3 cloves garlic, very finely chopped (optional)

a handful of fresh basil leaves, roughly chopped

about 18 cherry tomatoes

1. Cook the pasta according to package directions. Drain, rinse with cold water and set aside.

2. Meanwhile, steam the cauliflower florets in a vegetable steamer or saucepan until tender. Drain and set aside.

3. Preheat the oven to 400°F (200°C). Grease a baking dish—a transparent one (like Pyrex) is nice, so you can see the pasta browning underneath and on the sides.

4. Combine the cooked pasta with the melted margarine in the prepared baking dish.

5. Add the cauliflower and the remaining ingredients, including a good drizzling of olive oil, but reserving half the chopped basil and tomatoes. Mix well with a fork.

6. Even out the mixture in the dish and garnish with the rest of the basil leaves. Drizzle on some more olive oil, and bake for 20 minutes.

7. Remove from the oven and scatter the remaining tomatoes on top. Bake for another 20 minutes, until the casserole is a medium golden brown all over.

SPINACH & "RICOTTA" STUFFED PASTA SHELLS SERVES 4

IN MALTA, AS IN ITALY, we love our pasta. My mother used to stuff pasta shells with ricotta, and I've felt a little nostalgic for this dish. So I put on my vegan chef hat and started converting—substituting firm tofu for the ricotta, baking the pasta shells in soymilk and topping with a spicy tomato sauce. This has proved a winner for impressing non-vegan dinner guests.

FILLING

1 12-oz (340-g) package firm silken tofu

12 oz (340 g) vegan cream cheese
(French onion flavor is fun)

1 cup (250 mL) grated Vegan Mozzarella
(see page 253 or use purchased)

1½ cups (375 mL) chopped spinach
(thawed frozen spinach works well)

salt to taste

3 cloves garlic, very finely chopped

1½ Tbsp (22.5 mL) fresh flat-leaf parsley,
finely chopped

SHELLS

¾ lb (375 g) dried jumbo pasta shells
(conchiglioni)

plain soymilk, for baking

nutmeg, for dusting

TOMATO SAUCE

extra virgin olive oil

3–4 cloves garlic, finely chopped

1 fresh red chili, finely chopped (optional,
but a great touch)

1½ Tbsp (22.5 mL) tomato paste

1 tsp (5 mL) vegan margarine

6 fresh tomatoes, chopped, or a 14-oz
(398-mL) can

salt and pepper to taste

FILLING

1. Mash all the filling ingredients together in a bowl.

SHELLS

1. Preheat the oven to 350°F (180°C).

2. Using a teaspoon and clean fingers, stuff the filling into the shells.

3. Place the shells upright in a greased baking dish and pour in enough soymilk to cover them halfway. Dust a tiny amount of nutmeg on top and cover with aluminium foil.

4. Bake for 1½ hours, or until the shells are cooked. Remove the dish from the oven every 20 minutes or so to check and baste the shells with soymilk to keep them moist. Taste to check that they are ready.

5. While the shells are baking, make the tomato sauce (see recipe below) to pour on top.

SAUCE

1. Heat the olive oil in a medium frying pan set over low heat, and fry the garlic for 1 minute.

2. Add the chili (if using) and cook, stirring, for a few minutes, being careful not to let it burn.

3. Add the tomato paste and the margarine. Stir, cover and simmer for 10 minutes.

4. Add the tomatoes and cook for another 10 minutes, or until the mixture has reduced to a thickish sauce.

5. Serve on top of the baked, stuffed shells and enjoy!

NUTTY SPINACH, ZUCCHINI & PESTO LASAGNA SERVES 4

THIS LASAGNA IS QUITE EASY TO MAKE, and sublime in taste. It has a melt-in-your-mouth filling, a crunchy nut topping and a divine aroma. In fact, once you try this recipe, you will most likely continue to make it for the rest of your life. Serve with a crunchy green salad and a dry white wine, and enjoy!

TOMATO SAUCE

3 cups (750 mL) cherry tomatoes

4 cloves garlic

1 Tbsp (15 mL) agave or maple syrup

salt to taste

1 Tbsp (15 mL) tomato paste

TOMATO SAUCE

1. Place the sauce ingredients in a blender and process for 2 minutes, until thick and smooth.

2. Pour the sauce into a nonstick saucepan and simmer over low heat for 30 minutes, stirring occasionally. Set aside.

CREAMY PESTO SAUCE

3 Tbsp (45 mL) olive oil

2 large zucchini, sliced into circles

2 tsp (10 mL) vegan pesto (see page 77 or use purchased)

8 oz (250 g) frozen spinach, thawed

1½ cups (375 mL) vegan cream (see page 249 or use purchased)

1 Tbsp (15 mL) nutritional yeast, Nutty Parmesan (see page 262 or use purchased)

1 tsp (5 mL) garlic powder

salt to taste

TO ASSEMBLE

6 sheets dried lasagna

2–3 cups (500–750 mL) grated Vegan Mozzarella (see page 253) or other vegan cheese that melts

extra vegan cream, for topping

½ cup (125 mL) mixed almonds and sunflower seeds, crushed (see note)

NOTE: To crush the nuts and seeds, either pulse in a food processor or wrap in a cloth, set on a cutting board and pound them.

PESTO SAUCE

1. Heat the olive oil in a saucepan set over medium heat. Fry the zucchini slices until lightly golden on both sides.

2. Add the pesto and spinach and cook, stirring, for a couple of minutes.

3. Stir in the rest of the ingredients and simmer gently for 10 minutes, then set aside.

TO ASSEMBLE

1. Preheat the oven to 400°F (200°C). Grease an 11- x 7-inch (2-L) casserole dish.

2. Place 2 lasagna sheets at the bottom of the dish, making sure to cover the entire bottom (break the sheets into pieces if necessary) then layer ⅓ of the cheese on top.

3. Spoon about half the Creamy Pesto Sauce on top, cover with ⅓ of the cheese, then top with another layer of lasagna.

4. Repeat the same procedure, layering the remaining pesto sauce, cheese and lasagna noodles.

5. Pour all of the tomato sauce on top of the lasagna, making sure it seeps through the sides and edges by prodding the top layer gently with a knife.

6. Drizzle some cream in a zigzag pattern over the top, making sure that you can see the tomato sauce in between.

7. Sprinkle the nuts and seeds on top.

8. Bake for 45–50 minutes, until golden on top. Check the lasagna at this point—if it feels soft when you place a skewer in it, that means the pasta has softened, which is what you want. If not, return it to the oven for a few more minutes, then check again.

9. When the lasagna is cooked through, remove from the oven and leave to cool for at least 30 minutes before serving, so that it cuts well. Serve with a salad, if you wish.

STATE-OF-THE-ART LASAGNA

SERVES 4 GENEROUSLY

LASAGNA IS SUCH A VERSATILE DISH, and is there anyone who doesn't love it? This recipe pushes the boundaries of vegan lasagna, with juicy slices of eggplant, zucchini, mushrooms and peppers engulfed in a rich, creamy sauce. With its moist center, crunchy topping and flavor too tasty for words, this lasagna's aroma will knock you out as you take it out of the oven!

WHITE SAUCE

2 cups (500 mL) vegan cream (see page 249 or use purchased)

¼ cup (60 mL) nondairy milk (see page 249 or use purchased)

1 Tbsp (15 mL) nutritional yeast or Nutty Parmesan (see page 262 or use purchased)

LASAGNA FILLING

olive oil

1 large eggplant, thinly sliced lengthwise

2 medium zucchini, sliced lengthwise

2 green or red bell peppers, sliced lengthwise

3 cups (750 mL) of the best mushrooms you can get (I use porcinis), chopped

TOMATO SAUCE

olive oil

2 cloves garlic, finely chopped

2 Tbsp (30 mL) tomato paste

1 28-oz (796-mL) can diced tomatoes

¼ tsp (1 mL) ground cinnamon

½ tsp (2 mL) dried oregano

salt to taste

1 tsp (5 mL) agave or maple syrup

WHITE SAUCE

1. Combine all the ingredients in a mixing bowl and stir well. Set aside.

FILLING

1. Heat a drizzle of olive oil in a nonstick frying pan set over medium heat. Fry the eggplant slices until golden brown on both sides, then set aside.

2. Repeat for the zucchini slices, and set aside.

3. Add some more oil to the pan and gently sauté the bell peppers for about 2 minutes, ensuring that they remain al dente. Set aside.

4. Add some more oil, sauté the mushrooms for a few minutes and set aside (including their juices).

TOMATO SAUCE

1. Heat another drizzle of oil in the frying pan and sauté the garlic for about 20 seconds, then add the tomato paste. Stir well for about 20 seconds, then pour in half the tomatoes. Lower the heat, cover and cook for 10 minutes or so.

2. Add the rest of the tomatoes and the cinnamon, oregano, salt and agave or maple syrup and cook uncovered for about 20–30 minutes, until the sauce has reduced a little. You should be left with a thick, aromatic pulp. Turn off the heat and leave to cool for a few minutes.

6 sheets dried lasagna

3 cups (750 mL) roughly grated or sliced Vegan Mozzarella (see page 253) or other vegan cheese that melts

a handful of fresh basil leaves, chopped

1 cup (250 mL) raw almonds, roughly chopped

TO ASSEMBLE

1. Preheat the oven to 400°F (200°C) and grease an 11- x 7-inch (2-L) deep casserole dish.

2. Place a layer of lasagna sheets in the prepared casserole dish using 2 of the sheets. Make sure you cover the entire bottom—you can break some of the sheets into pieces to make them fit.

3. Spread the zucchini slices on top of the pasta. Top with 1 cup (250 mL) of the cheese.

4. Layer on the eggplant slices, then spoon over half the tomato sauce.

5. Add another layer of lasagna using 2 more sheets, then top with all of the mushrooms, including their juices.

6. Layer the peppers on top of the mushrooms, and sprinkle on another cup of cheese.

7. Top with another layer of lasagna using the last 2 sheets and the final cup of cheese.

8. Spread on the remaining tomato sauce and scatter the fresh basil on top.

9. Now drizzle on the white sauce, making sure that, as you pour it, you leave a few ½-inch (1-cm) gaps, so that the tomato sauce is peeking out. Sprinkle on the raw almonds.

10. Bake for 30 minutes, then remove the lasagna from the oven. Using a sharp pointed knife or skewer, pierce a few holes randomly on the surface, to allow the lasagna to breathe and distribute its juices. Return the dish to the oven, and bake for another 20–30 minutes.

11. Whatever you do, do NOT serve immediately—this dish will need at least 30 minutes to cool, otherwise it will not cut well. If you want to do something useful in the meantime, prepare a crisp green salad to complement this filling and delicious lasagna. *Bon appétit!*

TORTELLINI
with Creamy Wild Mushroom Sauce SERVES 4

TORTELLINI IS A FIRM FAVORITE IN THE MEDITERRANEAN. Though it's not always easy to find tortellini with a vegan filling, they are available—however, vegan ravioli will also do the job. The results are delicious, and easy as pie to make, too.

1½ lb (750 g) fresh vegan tortellini or ravioli

extra virgin olive oil

4 slices smoked vegan bacon, diced

1 zucchini, sliced

2 cups (500 mL) mixed wild mushrooms (dried, rehydrated ones will do), chopped

3 cloves garlic, finely chopped

2 cups (500 mL) vegan cream (see page 249 or use purchased)

salt to taste

a little nondairy milk (see page 249 or use purchased)

Nutty Parmesan (see page 262) or other vegan Parmesan, for garnish (optional)

fresh basil, chopped, for garnish

1. Cook the tortellini al dente, then rinse with cold water and set aside.

2. Heat a drizzle of olive oil in a nonstick saucepan set over medium heat. Fry the bacon until crisp, then set aside. Repeat with the zucchini, then fry the mushrooms and leave them in the pan.

3. Return the cooked bacon pieces to the saucepan with the mushrooms, adding the garlic at the same time. Cook over medium heat, stirring, for a couple of minutes.

4. Add the zucchini and cook, stirring, for another minute.

5. Stir in half the cream. Cook, covered, for 1 minute.

6. Salt to taste, and stir in a little milk if the sauce is too thick.

7. Toss in the tortellini, and mix well to coat with the sauce.

8. Serve immediately with a drizzle of extra virgin olive oil, a sprinkling of Nutty Parmesan, if you wish, and fresh basil leaves to garnish.

WILD STUFFED PASTA BALLS SERVES 4

THIS RECIPE CAME FROM AN INSPIRATION to create the opposite of spaghetti and meatballs—with the "meat" inside the pasta, rather than swimming around it. This is probably one of the most delicious pasta dishes I have ever tasted!

DOUGH

2 ¼ cups (560 mL) unbleached all-purpose flour

1 ¼ cups (310 mL) water, divided

FILLING

2 Tbsp (30 mL) olive oil

½ cup (125 mL) roughly chopped pecans

2 cloves garlic, chopped

1 tsp (5 mL) chili powder

1 tsp (5 mL) fine garlic granules

½ tsp (2 mL) dried oregano

2 ¼ cups (560 mL) hydrated TVP (see page xviii) or vegan ground meat substitute

8 oz (250 g) frozen spinach, thawed

½ cup (125 mL) vegan cream (see page 249 or use purchased)

¼ cup (60 mL) dry white wine

2 tsp (10 mL) vegetable stock granules

salt to taste

DOUGH

1. In a mixing bowl, combine the flour and ¾ cup (185 mL) of the water, and stir with a fork.

2. Add the remaining ½ cup (125 mL) of water, and mix with your hands until the dough is firm.

3. Wrap the dough in plastic wrap and refrigerate while you prepare the sauce.

FILLING

1. Heat the oil for a few seconds in a large nonstick saucepan set over medium heat. Fry the pecans for a minute or so, until they get some color.

2. Reduce the heat to low and add the garlic, then add the chili powder, garlic granules and oregano. Cook for 1 minute, stirring.

3. Add the TVP or ground meat substitute and cook for 5 minutes or so.

4. Add the remaining ingredients and cook for a few minutes, stirring constantly. Lower the heat to the minimum setting and cook for another 5–10 minutes, making sure the mixture doesn't stick.

5. Remove from the heat and cool.

(continued next page)

TOMATO SAUCE

2 Tbsp (30 mL) olive oil

3 cloves garlic, finely chopped

1 tsp (5 mL) chili powder

1 28-oz (796-mL) can diced tomatoes

1 tsp (5 mL) dried oregano

1½ tsp (7.5 mL) agave or maple syrup

salt to taste

TO ASSEMBLE

nondairy milk, for boiling the pasta balls

chopped fresh basil and grated vegan cheese, for garnish (optional)—use either Vegan Mozzarella (see page 253), Mild Cheddar "Cheese" (see page 254) or purchased

TOMATO SAUCE

1. Heat the oil in a nonstick saucepan set over medium heat, then fry the garlic and chili powder for 1 minute, stirring constantly.

2. Add half the tomatoes and cook for 10 minutes.

3. Add the rest of the tomatoes, together with the oregano and agave or maple syrup. Simmer gently, until the sauce reduces slightly, just over 10 minutes.

4. Salt to taste and then cook, stirring, for another minute or two before removing the sauce from the heat.

TO ASSEMBLE

1. Fill a large saucepan ¾ full with a mixture of 80% water and 20% milk, and place over medium–high heat. Preheat the oven to 400°F (200°C).

2. Roll the dough out onto a clean, floured surface, spreading it out as much as possible without thinning it too much to work with.

3. Using a teacup saucer (about 6 inches/15 cm in diameter) as an outline, cut out 5 circles.

4. Next, spoon a heaped tablespoon (about 20 mL) of the filling into the center of each circle, then twist the tops clockwise to seal them.

5. Once the water and milk mixture has come to a boil, add the balls to the saucepan and boil for 5 minutes.

6. Remove the balls with a large slotted spoon, and place them in a baking dish.

7. Pour the Hot Tomato Sauce on top, cover with aluminum foil and bake for 15 minutes.

8. Remove from the oven and serve immediately, garnished with basil and a sprinkle of grated cheese, if you wish.

STIR-FRIED VEGGIES
with Cashews & Noodles SERVES 4

THE ORIGINS OF STIR-FRYING DATE BACK THOUSANDS OF YEARS, to ancient China. This vegan stir-fry with cashews and rice noodles is a worthy continuation of the tradition—nutritious, and very easy to prepare. Little Chinese pots and chopsticks really do this dish justice. Feel free to add more soy sauce if you wish, and enjoy!

1 Tbsp (15 mL) sesame oil

24 whole raw cashews

1 carrot, thinly sliced lengthwise

1 long zucchini, sliced lengthwise

4 large mushrooms, finely chopped

1¼ lb (625 g) dried rice noodles

½ tsp (2 mL) turmeric

a handful of cabbage, sliced lengthwise

4 cloves garlic, finely chopped

1 medium onion, halved, then sliced lengthwise

½ green bell pepper, sliced lengthwise into strips

½ red bell pepper, sliced lengthwise into strips

1 tsp (5 mL) Chinese five-spice powder

3 Tbsp (45 mL) soy sauce

½ cup (125 mL) sweet chili sauce (see page xxi)

6 oz (175 g) firm silken tofu

1 cup (250 mL) canned or frozen corn (thawed)

1. Heat the sesame oil in a wok set over medium heat (don't let it burn).

2. Fry the cashews until they are lightly browned all over. Remove and set aside.

3. Add the carrot and zucchini to the wok and cook until they have some color.

4. Add the mushrooms and cook, stirring, for a few minutes, until they are soft.

5. While the mushrooms are cooking, cook the rice noodles according to package instructions (usually about 3 minutes in boiling water), adding the turmeric to the cooking water. Drain and set aside.

6. Add the cabbage to the wok and cook for a couple of minutes, stirring.

7. Add the garlic, onion, peppers and five-spice powder and continue to stir.

8. Add the cooked noodles and remaining ingredients and stir until well combined.

9. Sprinkle the cashews on top and serve immediately.

SPICY MOROCCAN PIZZA

SERVES 4 (MAKES TWO 12-INCH/30-CM PIZZAS)

THIS RECIPE WAS INSPIRED BY MY DEEP LOVE FOR PIZZA and by one of my favorite dips, the Moroccan Smoked Eggplant Dip (see the recipe on page 28). This pizza should have a light base—it's meant to be a thinnish, Italian-style oven-baked pizza. Note that you need to prepare the Moroccan Smoked Eggplant Dip in advance.

DOUGH

2 ¼-oz (7-g) packages quick-rising yeast

1 tsp (5 mL) sugar

1 cup (250 mL) water, at room temperature

2 cups (500 mL) unbleached all-purpose flour

1 cup (250 mL) whole wheat flour

1 tsp (5 mL) fine sea salt

1 Tbsp (15 mL) extra virgin olive oil

1 tsp (5 mL) garlic powder or finely chopped garlic

TOMATO SAUCE AND TOPPINGS

1 14-oz (398-mL) can diced tomatoes

6 or 7 cherry tomatoes, chopped

1 Tbsp (15 mL) tomato paste

4 Tbsp (60 mL) Moroccan Smoked Eggplant Dip (see page 28)

2 cloves garlic, chopped

6–8 black olives

½ tsp (2 mL) dried oregano

½ cup (125 mL) Vegan Mozzarella (see page 253 or use purchased)

extra virgin olive oil, for drizzling

DOUGH

1. Place the yeast and sugar in a bowl and add ¼ cup (60 mL) of the water. Let stand for about 15 minutes, or until the mixture starts to froth.

2. In a separate bowl, mix together both types of flour and the salt, making a well in the middle.

3. Pour the oil, garlic, yeast mixture and the rest of the water into the well. Stir with a wooden spoon to form a dough, and transfer the dough to a floured bowl.

4. Place a cloth over the bowl and leave the dough to rise in a warm place for about 30–40 minutes (it may need a little longer, depending on the temperature of the room). When it has doubled in size, it is ready for use. While the dough is rising, prepare the tomato sauce and the toppings.

QUICK METHOD FOR DOUGH:

To save time, process the yeast, sugar, flours and salt in a food processor for a minute or so. Slowly add the rest of the ingredients, and process until the dough forms into a ball. If the mixture is too dry, add a little more water, and if it is too wet, add a tiny bit of flour to be sure it stays in one piece. Transfer the mixture to a floured bowl and continue with step 4.

SAUCE AND TOPPINGS

1. Combine the canned tomatoes, cherry tomatoes and tomato paste in a glass bowl and set aside.

TO ASSEMBLE

1. Preheat oven to 425°F (220°C) and oil two 12-inch (30-cm) pizza trays.

2. Spread some flour on a completely clean surface and divide the dough ball in half. Flatten each half into shape using a rolling pin, making sure you dust flour on both sides to avoid sticking. Roll out the dough so the pizza bases are slightly larger than the trays. Carefully transfer onto the pizza trays and trim the excess dough from the edges.

3. Spread the tomato sauce evenly across the pizza bases, leaving 1 inch (2.5 cm) around the edges. Spread the Moroccan Smoked Eggplant Dip on top of the tomato sauce.

4. Distribute the garlic, olives and oregano evenly over the sauce, and sprinkle on half the cheese. Top with a drizzle of olive oil.

5. Bake the pizzas in the preheated oven for 15–20 minutes, until the crust is golden.

6. Sprinkle the pizzas with remaining cheese. Bake for another 5–10 minutes until the cheese melts, making sure to not let the pizzas burn.

7. Serve immediately with a nice green salad.

POLENTA GARDEN PIZZA

SERVES 4 (MAKES TWO 12-INCH/30-CM PIZZAS)

THIS PIZZA IS QUITE SIMPLY DELICIOUS. A cornmeal crust smeared with pesto and topped with fresh and sundried tomatoes, garlic scapes, spicy olives and a drizzling of extra virgin olive oil—glorious! You can use either my Parsley, Basil & Pecan Pesto (see the recipe on page 77) or a purchased vegan pesto.

DOUGH

2 ¼-oz (7-g) packages quick-rising yeast

1 tsp (5 mL) sugar

1 cup (250 mL) water, at room temperature

1½ cups (375 mL) cornmeal

1 cup (250 mL) unbleached all-purpose flour

½ cup (125 mL) whole wheat flour

1 tsp (5 mL) fine sea salt

1 Tbsp (15 mL) extra virgin olive oil

1 tsp (5 mL) garlic powder or finely chopped garlic

TOPPINGS

2 cups (500 mL) pesto (1 cup/250 mL per pizza)—use either Parsley, Basil & Pecan Pesto (see page 77) or purchased

2 large tomatoes, sliced

2 garlic scapes, chopped

4 cloves garlic, chopped finely

12 whole cherry tomatoes

½ cup (125 mL) sundried tomatoes, chopped

12–15 spicy green olives, pitted

olive oil, for drizzling

2 cups (500 mL) grated Vegan Mozzarella (see page 253 or use purchased)

DOUGH

1. Place the yeast and sugar in a bowl and add ¼ cup (60 mL) of the water. Let stand for about 15 minutes, or until the mixture starts to froth.

2. In a separate bowl, mix together the cornmeal, flours and salt, making a well in the middle.

3. Pour the oil, garlic, yeast mixture and the rest of the water into the well. Stir with a wooden spoon to form a dough, and transfer the dough to a floured bowl.

4. Place a cloth over the bowl, and leave the dough to rise in a warm place for about 30–40 minutes (it may need a little longer, depending on the temperature of the room). When it has doubled in size, it is ready for use. While the dough is rising, prepare the toppings.

TOPPINGS

1. Prepare each topping and have ready for assembly of the pizzas.

TO ASSEMBLE

1. Preheat the oven to 425°F (220°C) and oil two 12-inch (30-cm) pizza trays.

2. Spread some flour on a completely clean surface and divide the dough ball in half. Flatten each half into shape using a

rolling pin, making sure to dust flour on both sides to avoid sticking. Roll out the dough so the pizza bases are slightly larger than the trays. Carefully transfer onto the pizza trays and trim the excess dough from the edges.

3. Spread the pesto evenly across the bases, leaving 1 inch (2.5 cm) around the edges.

4. Distribute all of the tomatoes, garlic and olives evenly over the pesto. Top with a drizzle of olive oil.

5. Bake the pizzas in the preheated oven for 15–20 minutes, until the crust is golden.

6. Sprinkle the pizzas with the cheese and drizzle with some more olive oil. Bake for a further 5–10 minutes until the cheese melts, making sure to not let the pizzas burn.

7. Serve immediately and enjoy.

YUMMY CURRIED POTATO BURGERS MAKES ABOUT 8 BURGERS

ALOO GOBI, the Indian curry made with potatoes, cauliflower and spices, is a firm favorite in our household. So I decided to create some fast burgers based loosely on that wonderful dish. If you like potato curry, you are going to love these. Serve with Mayo from the Heavens (see the recipe on page 250) and a simple salad of greens and cherry tomatoes on the side. If you don't have time to make the mayo, then slap on the ketchup!

3 Tbsp (45 mL) frozen peas

2 Tbsp (30 mL) frozen corn

4 portions of instant mashed potatoes, or 4 medium potatoes microwaved until soft, then peeled

1 Tbsp (15 mL) vegan margarine

about ¼ cup (60 mL) nondairy milk (see page 249 or use purchased)

1½ tsp (7.5 mL) curry powder

salt to taste

1 medium carrot, grated

½ onion

2 cloves garlic

4 mushrooms

sprig of fresh mint

sprig of fresh rosemary

2 tsp (10 mL) nutritional yeast

1½ Tbsp (22.5 mL) unbleached all-purpose flour

olive oil

1. Place the peas and corn in a saucepan and cover with boiling water. Cook for a couple of minutes, then drain and set aside.

2. Meanwhile, in a medium bowl, prepare the instant mashed potatoes according to package directions (you may wish to substitute milk for some of the water) or mash the microwaved potatoes. Add the margarine, milk, curry powder and salt. Bear in mind that the mash needs to be a fairly firm consistency.

3. In a food processor, process together the carrot, onion, garlic, mushrooms and herbs.

4. Add the ingredients from the food processor to the mashed potato mixture, together with the cooked peas and corn, nutritional yeast and flour. Stir well with a fork, taste and adjust seasoning if necessary.

5. Heat a drizzle of olive oil in a nonstick frying pan set over medium heat. Spoon in dollops of the potato mixture. Cook for a few minutes, flattening very slightly with a spatula to make patty shapes, then gently flip. You may need to do this in batches, repeating with any remaining mixture, to make 8 burgers.

6. Serve on buns with your favorite burger fixings, or on their own with vegetables and salad. Reheat any leftovers in a hot oven—they may become mushy in the microwave.

NUTTY RED KIDNEY BEAN & QUINOA BURGERS MAKES 6 BURGERS

I HAVE BEEN MAKING VEGGIE BURGERS FOR YEARS, even before I became vegetarian—I've always loved them. These ones, combining red quinoa and red kidney beans, are very tasty indeed, not to mention incredibly nutritious and high in protein. They work very well served on fried slices of eggplant instead of buns, with a raw salad on the side, or on their own alongside rice and vegetables. They also freeze very well.

1 Tbsp (15 mL) soy sauce

1 Tbsp (15 mL) maple syrup

1½ tsp (7.5 mL) balsamic vinegar

½ cup (125 mL) red quinoa

1 cup (250 mL) water

1 medium potato or 1 cup (250 mL) prepared instant mashed potatoes

1 tsp (5 mL) vegan margarine

4 Tbsp (60 mL) olive or canola oil

1 medium red onion, finely chopped

1 tsp (5 mL) curry powder

3 cloves garlic, finely chopped

2½ Tbsp (37.5 mL) grated fresh ginger

4 Tbsp (60 mL) finely chopped fresh parsley

1 cup (250 mL) cooked red kidney beans (or canned, drained and rinsed)

1 cup (250 mL) mixed pecans and Brazil nuts, finely chopped

1 slice whole-grain bread, pulsed in food processor to make crumbs

salt to taste

zest and juice of ½ a lime

unbleached all-purpose flour, for dusting

1. To make the topping, stir together the soy sauce, maple syrup and balsamic vinegar in a cup and set aside.

2. Thoroughly rinse the quinoa, then place it in a small saucepan with the water. Bring to a boil, cover, lower the heat and simmer for 10–15 minutes, until the water is absorbed, being careful not to let the quinoa stick. Leave to cool.

3. Meanwhile, if you're using the whole potato, microwave it (in its skin) until soft, about 10 minutes. Peel and mash thoroughly. Alternatively, prepare the instant mashed potatoes according to package instructions if you haven't already done so.

4. Add the margarine to the mashed potatoes and mix until creamy and fluffy.

5. Heat 2 Tbsp (30 mL) of the oil in a frying pan set over medium heat. Sauté the onion and curry powder together for a few moments, stirring. Then add the garlic, ginger and parsley, and continue cooking and stirring for a minute or so. Remove from the heat.

6. Preheat the oven to 400°F (200°C).

7. In a large mixing bowl, mash the red kidney beans into a pulp.

8. Add the mashed potatoes, quinoa, onion mixture, nuts, breadcrumbs and salt to the mashed kidney beans and mix well. Add the lime zest and juice and mix again.

9. When all the ingredients are well blended, shape into 6 burgers with clean hands. First, roll into a ball in the palm of your hands, then flatten and place on a large, floured plate and refrigerate for at least 1 hour.

10. Heat the remaining 2 Tbsp (30 mL) of oil in a nonstick frying pan over medium heat, and fry the burgers in batches for about 5 minutes on each side, until browned.

11. Transfer the burgers to an ovenproof dish, and place in the preheated oven for 10 minutes. Remove from the oven, spoon on the topping and serve.

FAST LAYERED TOMATO CHEESE BURGERS MAKES 4 BURGERS

THESE BURGERS ARE VEGAN FAST FOOD—but without compromising on taste or texture. They are sort of a deconstructed cheeseburger: whole tomatoes layered with vegan burger patties, cheese and green onions, baked in the oven surrounded by veggies. I like to serve these with whole-grain bread to soak up the juices—an indulgent treat!

olive oil

4 purchased vegan burgers

2 zucchini, thinly sliced into rounds

2 cups (500 mL) sliced mushrooms

8 sundried tomatoes, chopped

3–4 cloves garlic, slivered

salt to taste

4 large tomatoes

8 medium-thick slices Vegan Mozzarella
(see page 253) or other vegan cheese
that melts

4 spring or green onions, sliced
lengthwise

a handful of fresh basil, plus extra for
garnish

1. Heat a drizzle of olive oil in a nonstick pan set over medium heat. Fry the burgers according to package directions, until they are cooked on both sides.

2. In a separate frying pan, heat another drizzle of oil, and sauté the zucchini slices for a few minutes per side, until lightly browned.

3. Stir in the mushrooms and cook for a few minutes, until they yield their juices, then add the sundried tomatoes, garlic and a sprinkle of salt. Cook for another minute, then remove from the heat.

4. Preheat the oven to 400°F (200°C). Prepare a large rectangular casserole dish that will fit the 4 tomatoes.

5. Make sure the bases of the tomatoes sit flat on their bottoms. If they don't, use a sharp knife to cut a thin slice from the bottoms, to ensure that they sit firmly without rocking.

6. Slice each tomato horizontally into 4 slices.

7. Place a thick slice of cheese on the first tomato layer, then top with the second piece of tomato. Place the cooked burger and slices of spring onion on the second layer. Top with the third tomato slice, then cover the last layer with another slice of cheese. Top with the final piece of tomato. Repeat with the remaining tomatoes.

8. Carefully place the stuffed tomatoes in the baking dish, and surround them with the zucchini and mushroom mixture.

9. Drizzle a little olive oil on the top of each tomato, toss in the fresh basil and bake in the preheated oven for 25 minutes, checking often to make sure they don't burn.

10. Transfer the tomatoes carefully to warm plates, surround with the veggies and all their juices and garnish with more fresh basil.

GOBSMACKED STICKY TOFU BURGERS MAKES 4–6 BURGERS

THIS HAS GOT TO BE ONE OF THE TASTIEST BURGERS EVER—they got their name because I was gobsmacked at the result. They're spicy and a little sweet, with an amazing texture—moist and slightly chewy. And the flavor is iconic: caramelized, succulent, satisfying, rich, irresistible—after one mouthful, you won't stop! (Kids adore them, too.)

---

2 oz (60 g) frozen spinach, thawed

1 cup (250 mL) arborio rice

3 cups (750 mL) water

½ tsp (2 mL) turmeric

9 oz (270 g) extra-firm silken tofu, thinly sliced

3 Tbsp (45 mL) teriyaki sauce (see page 127 or use purchased)

3 Tbsp (45 mL) soy sauce

2 Tbsp (30 mL) agave or maple syrup

1 Tbsp (15 mL) muscovado or dark brown sugar

1½ tsp (7.5 mL) plus 2 Tbsp (30 mL) olive oil, plus extra for frying

½ small onion, sliced into rings

2–3 cloves garlic, chopped

½ cup (125 mL) vegan ground meat substitute or hydrated TVP (see page xviii)

a pinch of chili powder

2 tsp (10 mL) brown sauce or HP sauce (optional)

1 cup (250 mL) medium-fine dried whole-grain breadcrumbs

salt to taste (optional—the soy sauce may give it enough salt)

1. First, ensure that the spinach is fully thawed, and then squeeze out the excess moisture through a sieve using either your hands or the back of a spoon.

2. Rinse the rice thoroughly and combine in a saucepan with the water and turmeric. Bring to a boil, cover, reduce the heat and simmer until the rice is cooked, about 30 minutes.

3. Meanwhile, cover a plate with paper towels and place the tofu slices on top, then cover with more paper towels. This will help absorb any excess water from the tofu.

4. Make the topping by combining the teriyaki sauce, soy sauce, agave or maple syrup, muscovado sugar and 1½ tsp (7.5 mL) of the olive oil with a fork. Set aside.

5. Dice the tofu into small pieces and place in a bowl. Spoon a little of the topping onto the tofu so that it absorbs the flavor and color.

6. Heat 2 Tbsp (30 mL) of the olive oil in a large nonstick frying pan set over medium heat. Fry the onion for 1–2 minutes, then add the garlic. Stir for 30 seconds, then add the ground meat substitute and cook for a minute or so.

7. Add the chili powder, followed by the diced tofu. Mix for a minute or so, then add the rice and spinach. Add the brown sauce (if using), and continue to stir until the rice browns and becomes a bit crispy.

chopped spring or green onions

lettuce leaves

sliced onion rings

8. Take off the heat, allow to cool for a few minutes, then transfer the mixture to a large bowl. Add the breadcrumbs and salt (if using), stir with a spoon and refrigerate for 1 hour.

9. Preheat the oven to 400°F (200°C). Using clean, slightly wet hands, shape the mixture into 4 to 6 patties and place on a tray or large plate lightly dusted with flour.

10. Heat a drizzle of oil in a frying pan set over medium heat. Fry the burgers for 3–4 minutes on each side, until nicely golden, then transfer them to an ovenproof dish.

11. Spoon 1 tsp (5 mL) or so of the tofu topping on each burger, and bake in the preheated oven for 10 minutes. Turn the burgers and spoon on some more topping, then return to the oven for another 10 minutes. Before serving, spoon any remaining topping on the burgers.

12. Garnish each burger with spring onions, a lettuce leaf and onion rings, and serve on a bun, or on its own.

MEDITERRANEAN QUINOA BURGERS with Sweet Pomegranate Sauce

MAKES 6 BURGERS

THIS RECIPE ROCKS—there's no better way to put it. The burger was designed for the sauce, and the sauce for the burger. The texture and nuttiness of red quinoa works beautifully in veggie burgers, and the sweet, spicy pomegranate sauce beats plain ketchup any day. This makes a nutritious and mouthwatering dinner, with a lovely combination of flavors. Make extra, because you're going to want to have these the next day, too.

BURGERS

1¼ cups (310 mL) red quinoa

2½ cups (625 mL) water

2 Tbsp (30 mL) sunflower seeds

2 garlic scapes or cloves, finely chopped

12 Greek black olives, pitted and chopped

2 shallots, finely chopped

2 cloves garlic, finely chopped

1 cup (250 mL) grated carrot

1 tsp (5 mL) hot curry powder

2 Tbsp (30 mL) chopped fresh flat-leaf parsley

2 Tbsp (30 mL) rolled oats

3 Tbsp (45 mL) ground flaxseed, mixed into a paste with 4 Tbsp (60 mL) water

2 Tbsp (30 mL) soy sauce

BURGERS

1. Combine the quinoa and water in a saucepan. Bring to a boil, cover and simmer for about 20 minutes, until the water is absorbed. Allow the quinoa to cool enough to handle.

2. Combine the cooked quinoa with the remaining ingredients in a large bowl, and using clean hands, shape into 6 burgers, flattening with your palms.

3. Place the burgers on a plate, cover and refrigerate until you're ready to fry them. In the meantime, prepare the sauce.

NOTE: Garlic scapes (also called stems or spears) can be found at Asian markets and farmers' markets in the spring and summer. If you can't find them, substitute garlic cloves.

(continued next page)

POMEGRANATE SAUCE

olive oil

1 small leek, finely chopped

1 medium zucchini, finely chopped

1 medium red bell pepper, finely diced

2 garlic scapes or cloves, finely chopped

1 Tbsp (15 mL) tomato paste

1 tsp (5 mL) paprika

1 14-oz (398-mL) can red kidney beans, drained and rinsed

1 cup (250 mL) pomegranate juice

1 14-oz (398-mL) can diced tomatoes

1 tsp (5 mL) agave or maple syrup (optional)

salt to taste

1 cup (250 mL) water

GARNISH

olive oil

lettuce or baby spinach leaves

sprigs of fresh flat-leaf parsley

slices of white onion

SAUCE

1. Heat a drizzle of oil for 1 minute in a nonstick saucepan set over medium–low heat.

2. Add the leek and zucchini and cook, stirring, for a couple of minutes.

3. Next, add the red bell pepper and garlic, and continue to stir for another minute or so—make sure not to burn your ingredients.

4. Add the tomato paste and paprika and cook, stirring, for another minute.

5. Add the kidney beans together with the pomegranate juice, tomatoes, agave (if using) and salt. Lower the heat and simmer, uncovered, for 20 minutes, or until the sauce thickens and reduces.

6. Add the water and return the sauce to a simmer. Cook gently for another 20 minutes, until the sauce reduces again. The result should be a thickish sauce, rich and aromatic. Remove from the heat and leave it to settle, covered.

TO COOK AND ASSEMBLE THE BURGERS

1. Heat a drizzle of olive oil in a nonstick frying pan over medium heat. Cook the burgers until browned on both sides, flipping them frequently, but making sure to handle them gently. Alternatively, you can bake the burgers for 30 minutes on a nonstick baking sheet in a 400°F (200°C) oven, flipping 2 or 3 times, until golden.

2. Serve on whole-grain seeded buns, with the pomegranate sauce smothered on top. Top with lettuce or baby spinach leaves, the parsley and slices of onion. Enjoy!

SUNRISE BURGERS MAKES 6 BURGERS

FULL OF FLAVOR AND EXTRA DELICIOUS, these golden burgers are a treat, and kids love them, too. The recipe came to me one day when I had way too much corn in my pantry, and too many sundried tomatoes in the fridge. These delights are wonderful served on a bed of rice, or in a whole-grain pita pocket with your favorite fixings, and a crunchy green salad on the side.

1¾ cups (435 mL) canned or frozen corn (thawed)

¾ cup (185 mL) yellow cornmeal

½ cup (125 mL) self-rising flour (see page xviii)

2 tsp (10 mL) egg replacer powder (see page xx)

½ tsp (2 mL) cornstarch

¼ tsp (1 mL) curry powder (optional)

¾ cup (185 mL) sundried tomatoes, chopped

1 large Spanish (or other mild, sweet) onion, finely chopped

1 cup (250 mL) grated vegan cheese that melts—use either Vegan Mozzarella (see page 253), Mild Cheddar "Cheese" (see page 254) or purchased

4 cloves garlic, finely chopped

¼ cup (60 mL) finely chopped fresh flat-leaf parsley

¼ cup (60 mL) grated carrot

salt and freshly ground black pepper to taste

olive oil

1. Place half the corn in a food processor, and process until smooth and creamy.

2. Combine the cornmeal, flour, egg replacer powder, cornstarch and curry powder in a large mixing bowl; stir to blend.

3. Add the processed corn, together with the remaining whole corn, and give it a good stir.

4. Finally, add the rest of the ingredients one at a time, and continue to stir until well blended. The mixture should have a nice thick consistency—if it's too runny, add a little more flour. Then refrigerate for 1 hour.

5. Preheat the oven to 325°F (160°C). Grease a baking sheet or other ovenproof dish large enough to hold 6 burgers.

6. Dust a large plate with flour, roll your sleeves up, wash your hands and roll enough of the mix in the palms of your hands to form a ball. Then flatten slightly into the shape of a burger and place on the dusted plate. Repeat with remaining mixture, to make 6 burgers in total. Place the burgers in the fridge for a few minutes.

7. Heat a drizzle of olive oil in a nonstick frying pan over medium–low heat, and fry the burgers for about 5 minutes, flipping them over once and then again a few moments later. Place the burgers on the prepared baking sheet and bake for 15 minutes.

8. Serve the burgers hot, topped with more grated cheese, if you like. Sweet chili sauce (see page xxi) is a favorite topping for these burgers.

WACKY HOT DOGS MAKES 5–6 SAUSAGES

MY OBJECTIVE HERE WAS TO CREATE A VEGAN FAST-FOOD CLASSIC—something to fill the void when the need for a quick carb fix arises. And unlike the unthinkable ingredients that make their way into processed meat products, all the ingredients in these hot dogs are healthy and nutritious. They were certainly a winner with my young daughter. Of course, you can buy ready-made vegan hot dogs, but making your own is so much more fun—and these are much tastier! Serve them on a toasted baguette with fresh lettuce, tomatoes, sliced onions and some yummy vegan mayo (see the recipe on page 250).

1¼ cups (310 mL) short-grain white or arborio rice

2 cups (500 mL) water

1 slice whole-grain bread, crusts removed

1 cup (250 mL) toasted hazelnuts

1 medium onion, roughly chopped

4 sprigs fresh flat-leaf parsley, leaves only

2 cloves garlic

1½ Tbsp (22.5 mL) flaxseed oil

2 Tbsp (30 mL) dry TVP, hydrated in 2 Tbsp (30 mL) water, or equivalent quantity of vegan ground meat substitute (see page xviii)

½ tsp (2 mL) smoked paprika

salt to taste

1 tsp (5 mL) prepared yellow mustard (hot is best)

1 tsp (5 mL) curry powder

2 tsp (10 mL) sweet chili sauce (see page xxi)

1 tsp (5 mL) muscovado or dark brown sugar

2 tsp (10 mL) unbleached all-purpose flour

2 Tbsp (30 mL) ground flaxseed

1 tsp (5 mL) flour mixed with 2 Tbsp (30 mL) toasted breadcrumbs, for coating

olive oil

GARNISH

lettuce leaves

sliced tomato

sliced onions

vegan mayo (see page 250 or use purchased)

1. Combine the rice and water in a saucepan and bring to a boil. Reduce the heat and simmer for 12–15 minutes, until the rice is cooked. Drain, rinse and set aside.

2. Meanwhile, process the slice of bread and the nuts in your food processor for 1 minute.

3. Add the onion and parsley, and process for another minute or so, using a spatula to move the ingredients to the center of the processor if needed.

4. Add the remaining ingredients except the rice, the extra flour and the toasted breadcrumbs for coating. Process for 2 minutes or so.

5. Finally, add the rice and process for another minute. At this point you should have a nice, thick mixture.

6. Sprinkle the flour and breadcrumbs onto a large plate. Using clean hands, form some of the sausage mixture into a ball. Roll out to create a sausage shape, place it on the plate and coat with the breadcrumb mixture, turning around to coat all sides. Repeat with the rest of the mixture, until you have 5 or 6 sausages.

7. Refrigerate the sausages for 1 hour.

8. Heat a drizzle of oil in a nonstick frying pan set over medium heat. Fry the sausages, turning them, until browned on all sides.

CURRIES

EGGPLANT, CHICKPEA, POTATO & COCONUT CURRY SERVES 4

THIS CURRY HAS STRONG THAI ORIGINS, since coconut is such a major player in Thai cuisine. Eggplant, which is so effective at absorbing juices, marries beautifully with the chickpeas, potato and spices. You could also substitute spinach for the eggplant. Try to find vegetarian "fish" sauce, which imparts a special flavor—I use Golden Mountain sauce (see "Vegan 'fish' sauce," page xxi). If you can't find it, soy sauce is an acceptable substitute.

about 5 Tbsp (75 mL) olive oil

1 medium eggplant, cubed

1 large onion, halved

6 cloves garlic

2 tsp (10 mL) grated fresh ginger

7 whole star anise

1 tsp (5 mL) curry powder

1 tsp (5 mL) ground cumin

½ tsp (2 mL) chili powder

1 tsp (5 mL) ground cardamom

1 large potato, cubed

1 14-oz (398-mL) can chickpeas, drained and rinsed

1 Tbsp (15 mL) Vegan "fish" sauce (see page xxi) or soy sauce

1 14-oz (398-mL) can coconut milk (not reduced-fat)

¼ cup (60 mL) water

2 tsp (10 mL) raw or turbinado sugar

salt to taste

finely chopped fresh cilantro, for garnish (optional)

1. Heat a drizzle of oil in a nonstick frying pan set over medium heat, and fry the eggplant for a few minutes, stirring frequently. When it has a little color on all sides, remove and set aside.

2. Place the onion, garlic and ginger in a food processor, and process until very finely minced.

3. Pour a little more olive oil into the pan, and fry the onion mixture over medium heat, stirring constantly. When it turns a little golden, add the star anise and the rest of the spices. At this point you will probably need to add a little more olive oil. Continue to mix well.

4. Add the remaining ingredients except the cilantro, lower the heat and cook for about 40 minutes. Alternatively, for a thicker consistency, simmer for 30 minutes, and then transfer to a covered casserole dish and place in a 300°F (150°C) oven for another 30 minutes or so. Whichever method you use, the consistency of the finished sauce should be on the thick side.

5. Garnish with some finely chopped fresh cilantro, if you like, or serve as is, with star anise smiling on the surface.

FASTEST THAI CURRY EVER

SERVES 4

I CHALLENGED MYSELF TO A VERY FAST CURRY, and the result was surprisingly superb. Once the ingredients are on your work surface, you can knock this out in 30 minutes—now that's a knockout. The taste is too good to be true, but find out for yourself. Don't skip the lemon-lime rice with sesame seeds, a perfect complement.

2 cups (500 mL) short-grain brown or
   white rice, or basmati rice

6 cups (1.5 L) water

sesame oil

1 eggplant, cut into large cubes

2 zucchini, sliced into rounds ¼ inch
   (0.5 cm) thick

1 large spring or green onion, finely chopped

2–3 cloves garlic, finely chopped

1½ tsp (7.5 mL) ground sumac

1 tsp (5 mL) peppercorns

½ tsp (2 mL) Chinese five-spice powder

½ tsp (2 mL) ground ginger

2 Tbsp (30 mL) crunchy peanut butter

2 Tbsp (30 mL) thick teriyaki sauce (see
   below or use purchased)

1 14-oz (398-mL) can coconut milk (not
   reduced-fat)

1 tsp (5 mL) rice vinegar

zest of 1 lemon

juice of 1 lime

sesame seeds, for garnish

1 Tbsp (15 mL) finely chopped fresh
   cilantro, for garnish

1. Combine the rice and water in a saucepan and bring to a boil. Cover and simmer until the rice is cooked (about 12–15 minutes for white rice and 30–40 minutes for brown). Then drain, rinse and set aside.

2. Meanwhile, heat a drizzle of sesame oil in a large saucepan set over medium heat. Fry the eggplant and zucchini until they get some color.

3. Add the onion and garlic and continue cooking until they too become golden.

4. Now get all your spices except the fresh cilantro and sprinkle them onto your veggies. Stir in a little extra sesame oil, too.

5. Add the peanut butter and teriyaki sauce, and lower the heat. Cook for about 10 minutes, so that the veggies suck the flavors in.

6. Add the coconut milk and rice vinegar, and simmer for 20 minutes.

7. Transfer the cooked rice to a serving dish. Stir in the lemon zest, and squeeze the lime juice overtop.

8. Serve the curry on top of the rice or on the side. Sprinkle with sesame seeds and fresh cilantro, and voilà!

TERIYAKI SAUCE   MAKES ABOUT 1½ CUPS (375 ML)

¼ tsp (1 mL) fine garlic granules

1 cup (250 mL) light soy sauce

1 cup (250 mL) mirin (Japanese rice wine)

1 Tbsp (15 mL) rice vinegar

3–4 Tbsp (45–60 mL) muscovado or dark
   brown sugar

½–1 cup (125–250 mL) water

1. Combine all the ingredients in a saucepan set over medium heat and bring to a simmer.

2. Cook until the sauce has reduced by half and is thick but pourable. Add more water if you want a thinner sauce, or more sugar if you like it sweeter.

3. Cool and store in an airtight jar in the refrigerator—it will keep for several weeks.

POTATO, PEA & SPINACH CURRY SERVES 4

THIS IS A TERRIFIC EVERYDAY CURRY—easy to make and very gratifying. I've kept the ingredients simple to bring out the satisfying flavor of the curry powder and cardamom—one of my favorite spices. This tastes great with homemade roti or poppadoms, basmati rice, some chutney and a tomato and raw onion salad.

---

2 medium potatoes

1 large onion

5 cloves garlic

2 tsp (10 mL) chopped fresh ginger

5 Tbsp (75 mL) extra virgin olive oil

2 tsp (10 mL) hot curry powder

½ tsp (2 mL) turmeric

¾ tsp (4 mL) ground cardamom

4 cardamom pods

1 tsp (5 mL) tikka paste (see page xxi)

1 cup (250 mL) frozen small peas

1 lb (500 g) frozen spinach, thawed

2 Tbsp (30 mL) sultana raisins

salt to taste

1½ cups (375 mL) water

1. Microwave the potatoes in their skins for about 12–15 minutes, until soft. Chop each potato into 4 or 5 pieces.

2. Place the onion, garlic and ginger in your food processor and process until finely chopped.

3. Heat the oil in a nonstick saucepan set over medium–low heat for a minute or so. Fry the onion mixture for a few minutes, stir in the spices except for the tikka paste and cook for another minute.

4. Add the potatoes to the saucepan and mix well, so they soak up the lovely flavors of the spices.

5. Add the tikka paste and cook, stirring, for another few minutes.

6. Add the remaining ingredients except the water and lower the heat. Cook for 5 minutes, stirring in the water a little at a time. Cover when you have added all the water.

7. Cook on low heat for 30 minutes, then serve.

ORANGE & CHOCOLATE KNOCKOUT CURRY SERVES 4

THIS UNIQUE RECIPE CAME TO ME ONE NIGHT when sleep had abandoned me, and the result the following day was a resounding success. Orange and chocolate may seem like unusual ingredients in a curry, but the combination of bittersweet and citric flavors, combined with the warmth of the curry spices and rounded out by the creaminess of coconut, is nothing short of inspiring. And the presentation—served in a whole pumpkin shell—is sure to impress. Serve with roti, basmati rice and a chopped green salad. I hope it brings you as much joy as it brought my family (including my five-year-old daughter).

---

1 medium pumpkin

1 large onion, roughly chopped

3 cloves garlic, each chopped into 3 or 4 pieces

1 green chili, chopped

1 1½-inch (4-cm) piece fresh ginger, peeled and roughly chopped

1 large sweet orange, peeled

olive oil

¼ cup (60 mL) olive or other oil, to mix with the spices

¼ tsp (1 mL) ground cinnamon

2 tsp (10 mL) hot curry powder

¼ tsp (1 mL) crushed cardamom seeds

1 tsp (5 mL) garam masala

¼ tsp (1 mL) turmeric

½ cup (125 mL) red lentils

2 Tbsp (30 mL) tomato paste

2 cups (500 mL) water

1 tsp (5 mL) orange zest

1 14-oz (398-mL) can red kidney beans, drained and rinsed well

10 oz (300 g) frozen spinach, thawed

1. Preheat the oven to 300°F (150°C) and grease an ovenproof dish large enough to hold the pumpkin.

2. To prepare the pumpkin, open the "lid" by slicing off the top 2 inches (5 cm) with a sharp knife. Cut away some of the flesh, taking care to keep the shell intact. Remove the pulp and seeds, discarding or saving for another use. Chop the removed pumpkin flesh into 1-inch (2.5-cm) pieces, and set them aside.

3. Replace the pumpkin lid and place the pumpkin shell in the prepared dish. Bake until it is almost scorched on top, and the flesh inside is fairly soft. Remove from the oven and set aside.

4. Meanwhile, place the onion, garlic, chili and ginger in the food processor and process until finely chopped. Transfer to a bowl and set aside.

5. Process the peeled orange in the food processor, and set aside in a separate bowl.

6. Heat a drizzle of oil in a nonstick saucepan set over medium heat. Fry the onion and garlic mixture until a little golden, but not burnt. Turn off the heat.

7. Combine the ¼ cup (60 mL) oil with all the spices in a small bowl, and stir until blended. Then turn on the heat to low, and add the spice mixture to the onion mixture, stirring for a minute or so. Enjoy the wonderful aroma that emerges.

(continued next page)

salt to taste (don't omit this as it will not be a balanced taste)

1 Tbsp (15 mL) agave or maple syrup

2 Tbsp (30 mL) finely chopped fresh cilantro

2 oz (60 g) nondairy dark chocolate— good-quality, with a high cocoa percentage

1½ cups (375 mL) coconut milk (not reduced-fat)

orange slices, for topping

8. Add the lentils, tomato paste and pumpkin cubes to the saucepan. Continue to cook, stirring, for a couple of minutes, making sure the heat is not too hot.

9. Add the water, bring to a simmer and cook until the lentils are soft, 30–40 minutes.

10. Add the remaining ingredients except the coconut milk and orange slices. Simmer very gently for 15 minutes, so that all the flavors have a chance to marry and mingle.

11. Add half the coconut milk, stir gently, then add the rest and cook for another15 minutes. The texture should be thick, and the taste a balance of savory and sweet.

12. Use a ladle to decant the curry into the pumpkin shell (if there is any leftover, it can be poured into the pumpkin for second helpings after the first batch is finished). Cover the pumpkin with its lid and return to the 300°F (150°C) oven for 10 minutes or so to allow the lid to cook a little.

13. Serve hot out of the oven—just remove the pumpkin lid and decorate the curry with slices of orange.

RED BOMB CURRY SERVES 4

THIS IS AN ADVENTUROUS CURRY INDEED—it has the perfect blend of salt, spice and sweetness, complemented perfectly by the velvety texture of the potatoes, the burst-in-your-mouth sultanas, and the moist, pungent sauce. In fact, it may be the most full-flavored, mouthwatering vegan curry ever!

4 medium potatoes

1 very large onion, roughly chopped

5 cloves garlic

1 2- to 3-inch (5- to 8-cm) piece fresh ginger, peeled and cut into 4 pieces

¼ cup (60 mL) extra virgin olive oil

2 tsp (10 mL) curry powder

1 tsp (5 mL) ground cumin

1 tsp (5 mL) garam masala

1 tsp (5 mL) chili powder

1 tsp (5 mL) coriander seeds

1 tsp (5 mL) crushed cardamom seeds (a must)

2–3 Tbsp (30–45 mL) tomato paste

2 cups (500 mL) vegan ground meat substitute or hydrated TVP (see page xviii)

¾ cup (185 mL) large sultana raisins

1 cup (250 mL) small green peas

2 cups (500 mL) water, plus extra as needed

chopped fresh cilantro, for garnish

1. Boil or microwave the potatoes in their skins until soft, then peel and chop each into 6 pieces.

2. Place the onion, garlic and ginger in your food processor and process until very finely chopped—almost liquid.

3. Heat the olive oil in a large nonstick saucepan (with a lid) over medium heat for a few seconds, then pour in the onion mixture. Lower the heat and cook for a few minutes, stirring almost constantly, as this mixture can burn easily.

4. Now add the spices, and stir for a few seconds. Add the tomato paste and the potatoes, and continue stirring over low heat for 1 minute.

5. Add the ground meat substitute, stirring continuously.

6. Add the raisins, peas and water. Cover and simmer gently for about 1 hour, keeping a careful eye on the curry to make sure it isn't sticking or getting too dry. Add a little more water if needed.

7. Serve hot, sprinkled wtih chopped cilantro, along with your favorite rice, poppadoms and a vegan raita. *Bon appétit!*

ROASTED EGGPLANT, MANGO & COCONUT CURRY

SERVES 4

THIS IS SUCH A SIMPLE CONCEPT, and yet so effective. Roasting the eggplant and zucchini creates another dimension of flavor, which, combined with the fresh, fruity bouquet of the mangoes and the aromatic lime zest, takes life to another plane! I garnish this delightful curry with some almonds and chopped bananas, and serve it with poppadoms and lightly spiced rice pilaf.

1 large zucchini, diced into 1-inch (2.5-cm) cubes

1 medium eggplant, diced into large cubes

olive oil

salt to taste

1 tsp (5 mL) ground cardamom

½ tsp (2 mL) ground coriander

½ tsp (2 mL) ground cumin

¾ tsp (4 mL) ground cinnamon

¾ tsp (4 mL) turmeric

½ tsp (2 mL) chili powder

1 tsp (5 mL) medium or hot curry powder

1 large onion, roughly chopped

1 1-inch (2.5-cm) piece fresh ginger, grated

½ tsp (2 mL) lemongrass powder (optional)

2 cloves garlic, finely chopped

2 cups (500 mL) thick coconut milk

1 Tbsp (15 mL) agave or maple syrup (optional)

2 cups (500 mL) mangoes, peeled, pitted and chopped into large pieces (make sure they are juicy and sweet)

zest of 1 lime

1. Preheat the oven to 375°F (190°C).

2. Place the chopped zucchini and eggplant in an ovenproof dish. Drizzle on some oil and sprinkle with salt, and bake for about 30 minutes.

3. Check if the veggies are ready by sticking a thin skewer in them—if there's no resistance, and if they have browned a little on the outside, they're ready. Turn off the heat, but leave them in the oven until your sauce is ready.

4. Meanwhile, heat a drizzle of olive oil in a saucepan set over medium–low heat. Fry the spices for 20 seconds or so, until they sizzle. Then add in the onion, stirring for a couple of minutes, followed by the ginger, lemongrass (if using), more salt to taste and garlic (be careful not to burn it).

5. Add 1 cup (250 mL) of the coconut milk, lower the heat and cook for 2 or 3 minutes.

6. Add the remaining coconut milk, and allow the mixture to simmer, but not boil, for 10 minutes.

7. Turn off the heat and leave the saucepan uncovered for a few minutes, then add the agave (if using), and blend with a handheld immersion blender until smooth.

8. Taste for salt, and add more if needed.

9. Turn on the heat to low, add the mangoes and lime zest, then the roasted veggies, and stir gently. Serve immediately.

SWEET POTATO FUSION CURRY SERVES 4

I CALL THIS A FUSION CURRY, because it has Indian, Thai and even African influences. Sweet potatoes, a vegetable I absolutely love, feature in both Asian and African cuisine, and as always with my curries, there is an inevitable debt of gratitude to Indian food. Serve with short-grain brown rice (mixed with a little vegan margarine and some cardamom), a green salad, poppadoms and a touch of mango chutney.

---

4 Tbsp (60 mL) extra virgin olive oil

1 medium onion, finely chopped

4 cloves garlic, finely chopped

1 1-inch (2.5-cm) piece fresh ginger, finely chopped or grated

1 small eggplant, cubed

2 zucchini, diced into medium-sized cubes

½ tsp (2 mL) Chinese five-spice powder

4 whole star anise

1 tsp (5 mL) crushed cardamom seeds or ground cardamom

1½ tsp (7.5 mL) hot curry powder

½ tsp (2 mL) lemongrass powder

5 mushrooms, sliced

2 Tbsp (30 mL) ground almonds

1 medium sweet potato, peeled and cut into 2-inch (5-cm) cubes

sea salt

2 tsp (10 mL) raw or turbinado sugar

2 cups (500 mL) coconut milk (not reduced-fat)

1 Tbsp (15 mL) sultana raisins

¾ cup (185 mL) canned or frozen corn (thawed)

a little water, if needed

1. Heat the olive oil in a large nonstick saucepan set over medium heat. Fry the onion, garlic and ginger in the oil for a few minutes, stirring.

2. Add the eggplant and zucchini, mix well and continue to cook, stirring, until the veggies begin to soften.

3. Stir in the spices, then add the mushrooms and ground almonds. Mix well, lower the heat and leave to cook for a few more minutes, covered, until the mushrooms have also softened.

4. Now stir in the sweet potatoes. Then add the remaining ingredients and cook, covered, over low heat for at least 1 hour. Make sure all the veggies are cooked through and soft, and that the sauce has slightly thickened (you may need to add a little more water if it's too thick). Serve over rice.

LENTIL & SPINACH TANDOORI MASALA

with Spicy Zesty Curried Potatoes SERVES 4

THIS IS A RELATIVELY QUICK CURRY TO MAKE, and it goes perfectly with the Spicy Zesty Curried Potatoes—a wonderfully warming and delicious combination.

SPICY ZESTY CURRIED POTATOES

1 large onion, finely chopped

1 2-inch (5-cm) piece fresh ginger

2 fresh red chilies

4 cloves garlic

olive oil

1½ tsp (7.5 mL) hot curry powder

3–4 medium potatoes, peeled and diced

salt to taste

1½ tsp (7.5 mL) coriander seeds

¾ tsp (4 mL) caraway seeds

zest of 1 orange, finely chopped

CURRIED POTATOES

1. Place the onion, ginger, chilies and garlic in your food processor, and process until finely chopped (this mixture will be used for both the potatoes and the curry sauce).

2. Preheat the oven to 400°F (200°C).

3. Drizzle some olive oil into a medium-sized casserole dish.

4. Smear 1 Tbsp (15 mL) of the processed onion mixture on the bottom of the dish, then sprinkle the curry powder evenly overtop. Roll the potatoes in the mixture, coating them well.

5. Add some salt, and evenly sprinkle the coriander seeds, caraway seeds and orange zest over the potatoes. Drizzle some more oil on top, and place in the preheated oven for about 1 hour, or until the potatoes are crusty on the outside, and nice and soft on the inside. Do keep an eye on them, though, as different potatoes require more or less time to cook. Meanwhile, make the curry.

(continued next page)

TANDOORI CURRY

olive oil

1 tsp (5 mL) curry powder

1 tsp (5 mL) coriander seeds

1 tsp (5 mL) caraway seeds

1 tsp (5 mL) garlic granules

1 tsp (5 mL) turmeric

½ tsp (2 mL) ground cumin

1 tsp (5 mL) ground cardamom

under ¼ tsp (1 mL) asafoetida powder
  (see note on page 141)

2 cups (500 mL) cooked or canned brown
  or red lentils

8 oz (250 g) frozen spinach, thawed

2 Tbsp (30 mL) ketchup

2 tsp (10 mL) tandoori paste

salt to taste

1 tsp (5 mL) agave or maple syrup

2½ cups (625 mL) coconut milk (not
  reduced-fat)

juice of 1 tangerine or orange

a few drops natural red food coloring

chopped nuts, for garnish (optional)

1 mango, peeled, pitted and chopped

TANDOORI CURRY

1. Heat a drizzle of olive oil in a large nonstick pan over medium–low heat, and gently fry the remainder of the processed garlic, onion, ginger and chili mix for about 5 minutes, stirring frequently.

2. Stir in all the dry spices, followed by a little more olive oil.

3. Add the cooked lentils and spinach.

4. Stir in the ketchup and tandoori paste.

5. Add some salt and the agave or maple syrup, and continue to cook for about 10 minutes over low heat.

6. Finally, add the coconut milk, tangerine or orange juice and food coloring. Cook for another 20 minutes over low heat, or place in a dish in a 375°F (190°C) oven for 20–30 minutes.

7. Garnish with chopped nuts, if desired, and serve alongside the potatoes with fresh mango, cooked rice, if you wish, and poppadoms.

FRUIT & VEG CURRY PIE SERVES 4

EAST AND WEST MARRY IN THIS DELICIOUS PIE. Eggplant and zucchini are the main veggies, with the prunes and spices adding the exotic touch, and all are contained in a traditional puff-pastry pie. This is a vegan delight to savor. Serve with a salad of mixed greens, tossed with Mayo from the Heavens dressing (see the recipe on page 250).

olive oil

1 small or medium eggplant, diced small

2 zucchini, chopped

1 large onion

3 cloves garlic

¼ tsp (1 mL) turmeric

½ tsp (2 mL) crushed cardamom seeds or ground cardamom

1 tsp (5 mL) garlic granules

1½ tsp (7.5 mL) hot curry powder

¼ tsp (1 mL) asafoetida powder (see note)

½ tsp (2 mL) coriander seeds

1 tsp (5 mL) ground cumin

about 8 prunes, chopped

1 Tbsp (15 mL) sultana raisins

1 tsp (5 mL) vegan brown sugar

1 Tbsp (15 mL) chopped fresh cilantro

5 cherry tomatoes, halved

salt to taste

¾ cup (185 mL) water, plus extra as needed

vegan puff pastry for 4 servings (about 1 lb/500 g)

1. Heat a drizzle of olive oil in a nonstick pan set over medium–low heat. Toss in the eggplant and zucchini and stir.

2. Process the onion and garlic together in your food processor until very finely chopped. Add them to the pan with the eggplant and zucchini.

3. Stir in the spices one at a time—you may need to add a little more oil if the mixture is drying up, which it has a tendency to do. Cook for 10 minutes or so, until all the veggies are soft.

4. Add the remaining ingredients except the water and pastry, cover and cook for another few minutes.

5. Add the water a bit at a time, mix and cook for about 20 minutes.

6. In the meantime, preheat the oven to 400°F (200°C) and grease an 8-inch (20-cm) round pan.

7. Divide the pastry into 2 portions, one larger than the other. On a floured surface, roll out the larger piece and press it into the prepared pan so it covers the base and sides. Trim the excess pastry from around the edges.

8. Carefully pour the curry onto the puff pastry bottom, then roll out the remaining pastry and place it on top, pressing the edges to seal them together. Bake for about 25 minutes, or until the top is golden. Cut into slices and serve.

NOTE: Asafoetida powder, also called *hing*, is a crucial ingredient in Indian cooking. It is sold as a fine yellow powder and is available in Indian markets. You only need to use a small amount, as its flavor is strong.

TANDOORI KOFTA MASALA

SERVES 4

TANDOORI HAS A UNIQUELY DELICIOUS FLAVOR—tangy, creamy, smoky and hot. This recipe combines a rich tandoori masala sauce with a vegan interpretation of kofta balls (traditionally made using ground meat). The result prompted my husband to pronounce it "genius food." Serve over hot basmati rice with poppadoms and a simple salad of finely chopped onions, tomatoes, cucumber and fresh cilantro.

KOFTAS

1 cup (250 mL) mixed nuts (cashews, almonds, brazil nuts—raw or roasted)

1 small onion, quartered

a handful of fresh cilantro

2 vegan beef-style burgers

1 small green chili

a handful of raisins

1 tsp (5 mL) tandoori paste

1 tsp (5 mL) curry powder

¾ tsp (4 mL) turmeric

½ tsp (2 mL) crushed cardamom seeds

½ tsp (2 mL) ground cumin

½ tsp (2 mL) sea salt

3 Tbsp (45 mL) olive oil

KOFTAS

1. Place the nuts in a food processor and process to fine crumbs, then transfer to a bowl.

2. Place the onion and cilantro in the processor, process until finely chopped and set aside in a separate bowl.

3. Place the vegan burgers in the processor and pulse a couple of times to chop.

4. Add the chili, raisins, tandoori paste, spices and salt, and process for about 20 seconds, until broken down.

5. Return the ground nuts and the onion mixture to the processor, and pulse until all the ingredients merge together. The mixture should be of a very thick consistency so you can form it into balls.

6. Spoon the mixture into a large bowl and refrigerate for 1 hour—this will make it easier to form the balls without too much mess and stickiness.

7. Shape the chilled mixture into balls (about 8 in total), and place them on a plate dusted with flour.

8. Preheat the oven to 400°F (200°C).

9. Heat the olive oil in a nonstick frying pan set over medium–low heat, and fry the balls until they get some color, turning them gently by shaking the pan. After 10 minutes or so, they should be cooked.

10. Transfer the koftas to a casserole dish and bake in the preheated oven for 15 minutes.

11. Remove from the oven and allow to cool. The koftas are now ready to be immersed in the tandoori masala sauce.

(continued next page)

SAUCE

1 large onion

4 cloves garlic

1 1-inch (2.5-cm) piece fresh ginger

2 green chilies, roughly chopped

1 tsp (5 mL) coriander seeds

1 tsp (5 mL) tandoori masala powder

1 tsp (5 mL) curry powder

1 tsp (5 mL) garam masala

¾ tsp (4 mL) ground cinnamon

½ tsp (2 mL) turmeric

½ tsp (2 mL) cumin powder

¼ cup (60 mL) olive oil, plus extra for frying

4 tsp (20 mL) tandoori paste

1 cup (250 mL) plain nondairy yogurt or vegan cream (see page 249 or use purchased)

8 oz (250 g) frozen spinach, thawed

1 14-oz (398-mL) can coconut milk (not reduced-fat)

1–2 Tbsp (15–30 mL) agave or maple syrup

1–2 tsp (5–10 mL) sea salt

TO ASSEMBLE

1 small red bell pepper, diced

SAUCE

1. Place the onion, garlic, ginger and chilies in a food processor and process until they are chopped very finely. This will be the base for the curry sauce.

2. To make the sauce mixture, place all the spices in a glass bowl, add the ¼ cup (60 mL) of olive oil and mix into a paste. Stir in the tandoori paste. Then add the yogurt and mix again. Set aside.

3. Heat a drizzle of oil in a large nonstick pan set over medium heat. Add the onion mixture and fry for a few minutes, pressing the mixture down with a wooden spoon. Add the sauce mixture and stir for a couple of minutes over low heat. Enjoy the aroma as it permeates your kitchen and beyond.

4. Add the spinach and half the coconut milk and stir. Lower the heat to minimum and allow to cook for 10 minutes.

5. Add the remaining coconut milk, agave and salt, and cook for another 10 minutes.

TO ASSEMBLE

1. While the sauce is thickening, preheat the oven to 250°F (120°C).

2. Pour the sauce into a small but deep casserole dish, then gently lower the cooked kofta balls one by one into the sauce, making sure each is fully covered in sauce. Gently stir in the red pepper. Cover the dish and bake for 20 minutes.

3. Remove from the oven and serve immediately over rice.

NOTE: Tandoori masala powder is available in Indian grocery stores.

VALENTINE KOFTA MASALA

SERVES 4

THESE WONDERFUL AND UNIQUE KOFTA BALLS have a crunchy, creamy paneer flavor (paneer is a mild Indian curd cheese), with a contrasting spicy, semi-sweet sauce to tease the taste buds and satisfy all the senses. The delicate spinach rounds out the flavors perfectly. The result is an exotic, delicious curry, ideal for creating a special mood of love, warmth and contentment. What's more, this recipe is relatively easy to make.

(continued next page)

KOFTAS

¼ cup (60 mL) unsalted pistachios

1 tsp (5 mL) edible dried rose petals (optional—see note)

1 cup (250 mL) mixed nuts (cashews and almonds work well)

1 14-oz (398-mL) can chickpeas, drained and rinsed

½ tsp (2 mL) curry powder

salt (without salt, it will taste like a dessert)

3 Tbsp (45 mL) plain vegan cream cheese

1 Tbsp (15 mL) finely chopped fresh parsley or cilantro

zest of 1 lime

juice of ½ lime

olive oil

2 cups (500 mL) brown or white basmati rice

6 cups (1.5 L) water

KOFTAS

1. Preheat the oven to 400°F (200°C). Line a baking sheet with parchment paper and grease the paper.

2. Make the coating for the koftas by processing the pistachios and rose petals (if using) in a coffee grinder or food processor until crumbs are formed. Transfer the crumbs to a bowl and set aside.

3. Place the mixed nuts in your food processor and process until rough crumbs form.

4. Add the chickpeas and pulse again a few times.

5. Now add the remaining ingredients except the oil, rice and water, and pulse for a few moments—you want a very thick consistency, like dough. Remove the mixture from the food processor, form into a ball and place on a lightly floured surface.

6. Pour some oil in a little saucer and rub some on the palms of your hands. Then pinch about a 1½-inch (4-cm) ball of the chickpea mix, roll it in the palms of your hands and place on a plate. Repeat this process until you have made approximately 12 balls, making sure they are a little oily so the pistachio and rose coating will adhere to them.

7. Roll each ball in the pistachio and rose mixture, until it's well coated. Place the coated balls on the prepared baking sheet.

8. Bake for 25 minutes or so, until the balls turn golden (since ovens vary so much, do keep an eye on them). Once they are ready, take them out of the oven and set aside.

9. Meanwhile, combine the rice and water in a saucepan. Bring to a boil, cover, and simmer until tender (about 15–20 minutes for white rice and 30–40 minutes for brown). Drain the excess water and set aside.

SAUCE

1 onion, quartered

2 cloves garlic

2 Tbsp (30 mL) unsweetened coconut oil, plus extra as needed

¼ tsp (1 mL) ground ginger

¼ tsp (1 mL) turmeric

¼ tsp (1 mL) crushed cardamom seeds or ground cardamom

1 tsp (5 mL) curry powder

½ tsp (2 mL) garam masala

2 tsp (10 mL) tikka paste (see page xxi)

1 lb (500 g) frozen spinach, thawed

3 Tbsp (45 mL) agave or maple syrup

salt to taste (it will need 1–2 tsp/ 5–10 mL)

1 cup (250 mL) water

1 cup (250 mL) coconut milk

1 tsp (5 mL) natural red food coloring

1 tsp (5 mL) rose essence

1 cup (250 mL) vegan cream (see page 249 or use purchased)

fresh lime juice

SAUCE

1. Pulse the onion and garlic in your food processor until finely chopped.

2. Heat the coconut oil in a saucepan set over medium heat. Fry the onion and garlic, stirring constantly.

3. When the onion has turned transparent, add the spices and tikka paste and continue to stir. You will probably need to add a little more oil at this point.

4. Add the remaining ingredients except the cream and lime juice. Lower the heat and simmer for 30 minutes, stirring occasionally so it doesn't stick or burn.

5. Finally, add the cream, and leave the sauce uncovered until it reduces and thickens. Don't allow it to boil or separate— you'll need to keep the heat low to avoid this.

6. When the sauce is ready, leave it uncovered until it cools, then cover.

7. To serve, carefully make a bed of cooked basmati rice in an ovenproof serving dish. Pour the sauce in the center and place the balls around the edges of the rice, then squeeze plenty of fresh lime juice on top of everything. *Voilà*—a feast for the eye, palate and soul!

NOTE: **Look for edible dried rose petals in gourmet specialty stores, Indian or Middle Eastern stores, or online.**

MOUTHWATERING
MAINS

CHILI CON "CARNE" SERVES 4

I LOVE CHILI—and without the carne, it's even better. This one scores high on both taste and nutrition. It is satisfying, easy to make and so very full of flavor. For the "carne," you can use a ready-made vegan ground "beef" substitute, vegan burgers or hydrated TVP (see page xviii). Serve with Soured Mint Cream (see the recipe below), and Winner Cornbread (see page 36).

CHILI

olive oil

1 large onion, finely chopped

5 cloves garlic, chopped

2 cups (500 mL) vegan ground meat substitute, hydrated TVP (see page xviii) or finely chopped vegan burgers

2 Tbsp (30 mL) tomato paste

1 tsp (5 mL) sweet paprika

½ tsp (2 mL) chili powder

½ tsp (2 mL) coriander seeds (optional)

½ tsp (2 mL) dried oregano

1 14-oz (398-mL) can diced tomatoes or 2 cups (500 mL) cherry tomatoes

1 14-oz (398-mL) can red kidney beans, drained and rinsed

1 tsp (5 mL) vegan brown sugar

salt and freshly ground black pepper to taste

½ green bell pepper, finely chopped

¼ cup (60 mL) water

SOURED MINT CREAM

½ cup (125 mL) vegan cream (see page 249 or use purchased)

½ cup (125 mL) plain nondairy yogurt

1 Tbsp (15 mL) finely chopped fresh mint or 2 tsp (10 mL) dried mint

1 Tbsp (15 mL) freshly squeezed lemon juice

a few drops extra virgin olive oil (optional)

a little lemon zest

salt and freshly ground black pepper to taste

CHILI

1. Heat a drizzle of oil in a nonstick frying pan set over medium heat. Fry the onion and garlic, but don't allow it to stick or burn—a minute or two should do the trick.

2. Add the ground meat substitute, stirring it around a little.

3. Keep stirring while you add the tomato paste, then the spices and herbs. Reduce the heat to low and cook, covered, for 30 seconds

4. Add the tomatoes, beans, sugar, and salt and pepper. Cover and cook over low heat for about 45 minutes, stirring occasionally.

5. Add the green pepper and the water, and continue to cook for a few more minutes. The green pepper will cook in the heat of the mixture, retaining a little crunch for texture.

6. Serve topped with Soured Mint Cream with cornbread on the side.

SOURED MINT CREAM

1. Combine all the ingredients in a bowl and mix together well using a fork. Spoon over the chili. This cream also works well on baked potatoes.

JUICY BURGER & POTATO STEW

SERVES 4

THIS DINNER IS A WINNER—reminiscent of a traditional beef stew, but even richer and tastier with the addition of extra garlic and spices. It's so easy and fast to prepare, great for the winter months and also a favorite with kids (though you may want to omit the fennel seeds). Serve with steamed veggies, or with a crunchy baguette and a green salad.

3 Tbsp (45 mL) extra virgin olive oil

1 large onion, finely chopped

3 large cloves garlic, finely chopped

2 large potatoes, halved, then sliced ½ inch (1 cm) thick

2½ Tbsp (37.5 mL) tomato paste

¾ tsp (4 mL) turmeric

½ tsp (2 mL) paprika

just under ¼ cup (60 mL) water, plus extra as needed

4 vegan burgers, gently fried on both sides

salt and freshly ground black pepper to taste

½ tsp (2 mL) fennel seeds, for sprinkling

1. Heat the oil in a saucepan set over medium heat. Fry the onion for 1 minute, stirring constantly. When it turns a little transparent, add the garlic and cook for another minute, being careful not to burn it.

2. Add the potatoes and tomato paste and cook, stirring, for a couple of minutes.

3. Stir in the turmeric, paprika and water. Cover and cook for 15 minutes.

4. Add the burgers (whole), lower the heat and cover. Cook until the potatoes are soft (be patient—it won't taste as good if the potatoes are still hard). The final consistency should be neither dry nor too saucy. If it seems too dry, add a little more water. If it's swimming in juices, simmer uncovered for a few more minutes, until some of the liquid cooks off.

5. Sprinkle on the fennel seeds and serve hot.

GREEK GARLIC BEAN STEW

SERVES 4

THIS IS THE PERFECT DISH to warm you from the inside out on a cold winter's day. My mother's Greek bean stew was an all-time favorite around our table in the winter months, and my updated version, with some different ingredients and a kick of heat, will really get the fires burning. Your immune system will thank you for this and, as a bonus, it is very easy and fast to prepare. Accompany with Chili Olive, Garlic & Rosemary Bruschetta (see the recipe on page 32)—a feast of fire awaits!

extra virgin olive oil

2 medium onions, finely chopped

2 large carrots, sliced into rounds ½ inch (1 cm) thick

2 large sweet potatoes, cut into 1-inch (2.5-cm) cubes

6 cloves garlic, finely chopped

12 whole cherry tomatoes

3 Tbsp (45 mL) tomato paste

1 tsp (5 mL) ground cinnamon

4 cups (1 L) vegetable stock

2 4-oz (398-mL) cans cannellini beans, drained and rinsed

2 tsp (10 mL) chili powder (or to taste)

2 Tbsp (30 mL) fresh celery leaves, finely chopped

2 tsp (10 mL) vegan margarine

salt to taste

1. Heat a drizzle of olive oil in a nonstick saucepan set over medium heat. Fry the onions, carrots and sweet potatoes for 3–4 minutes, stirring.

2. Add the garlic and continue to stir for a couple of minutes (making sure not to burn the garlic).

3. Add the cherry tomatoes and tomato paste and cook, stirring, for another minute.

4. Add the remaining ingredients, bring to a simmer and then lower the heat. Cover and simmer for 40 minutes, stirring occasionally.

5. The stew is ready when the veggies are soft. Serve hot and enjoy!

SUNDRIED TOMATO, BEAN & PASTA STEW SERVES 4

EAST-WEST FUSIONS CAN BE TRICKY, but this hot pot gets the combination perfectly right: each ingredient blends beautifully with its neighbor. Sundried tomatoes and coconut? It may sound unlikely, but taste and see for yourself—you'll probably end up making this time after time. All you need to complete the meal is some crunchy garlic bread.

---

4 Tbsp (60 mL) olive oil

1 medium onion, finely chopped

2 cups (500 mL) fresh pumpkin or other winter squash, peeled and cut into 1-inch (2.5-cm) cubes

2–3 Tbsp (30–45 mL) tomato paste

3 cups (750 mL) water

3 cloves garlic, slivered

4 sundried tomato halves, roughly chopped

2 cups (500 mL) cooked or canned cannellini beans, drained and rinsed

1 cup (250 mL) thick coconut milk

½ tsp (2 mL) turmeric

½ tsp (2 mL) curry powder

1 red bell pepper, thinly sliced

1½ cups (375 mL) dried fusilli (spiral pasta)

salt to taste

finely chopped fresh flat-leaf parsley, for garnish

1. Heat the olive oil in a medium-large saucepan set over medium heat. Sauté the onion and pumpkin for a few minutes, stirring frequently to avoid sticking or burning.

2. Add the tomato paste and continue stirring for 1 minute. Add a little more olive oil if the vegetables start to stick.

3. Add the water, bring to a simmer then reduce the heat and cook for 15 minutes or so, until the pumpkin has begun to soften.

4. Stir in the garlic, sundried tomatoes and beans, and simmer for another 15 minutes.

5. Add the coconut milk and spices, and simmer over very low heat for another 15 minutes.

6. Add the red pepper and simmer for another 5 minutes.

7. Add the pasta and salt to taste. Cook for 8–10 minutes, until the paste is al dente.

8. Serve hot, garnished with parsley.

STROGANOFF SUPREME SERVES 4

THIS STROGANOFF IS VERY EASY TO MAKE. I use sliced vegan burger instead of beef (you could also use vegan "beef" strips) and some wonderful button mushrooms. The result is an astounding success, with a sauce that compels you to eat more and more. Serve over steamed rice, broad noodles or even fries.

2 Tbsp (30 mL) olive oil

2 cups (500 mL) vegan burger sliced into strips, or vegan "beef" strips

1 small onion, finely chopped

2 cloves garlic, finely chopped

about 20 button mushrooms, roughly chopped

salt and freshly ground black pepper to taste

3 Tbsp (45 mL) soy sauce

1 tsp (5 mL) coriander seeds

a pinch of nutmeg

1 tsp (5 mL) pumpkin pie spice

2 tsp (10 mL) vegetable stock powder

1 Tbsp (15 mL) unbleached all-purpose flour

2 Tbsp (30 mL) sherry

1 cup (250 mL) vegan cream (see page 249 or use purchased)

chopped fresh flat-leaf parsley, for garnish

1. Heat 1 Tbsp (15 mL) of the oil in a large saucepan set over medium heat and cook the vegan burger slices or "beef" strips until browned on all sides. (Alternatively, you could grill them.) Set aside.

2. Heat the remaining oil in the saucepan and fry the onion and garlic for a couple of minutes, taking care not to burn them.

3. Add the mushrooms, cover the saucepan and allow them to sweat for 5 minutes or so, stirring occasionally.

4. When the mushrooms have yielded their juices, add the remaining ingredients except the sherry, cream and parsley. Continue to stir for a minute or so, then lower the heat and cook for another 10 minutes.

5. Add the sherry and cook for 5 more minutes.

6. Add the cream and the burger pieces. Cook over low heat for a few more minutes, until the sauce has thickened. Serve on top of rice or broad noodles.

BEAN GOULASH SERVES 4

THIS GOULASH IS WHOLESOME, flavorful and filling, with contrasting textures and the aromas of paprika, coriander and bay leaf. Served with rice or baked potatoes and salad and my quick and easy Soured Mint Cream (see the recipe on page 151), it makes a great dinner to share with non-vegan friends and family.

about 4 Tbsp (60 mL) olive oil

2 red onions, finely chopped

2 spring or green onions, finely chopped

4 cloves garlic, finely chopped

5 vegan burgers, vegan "beef" strips or hydrated TVP chunks (see page xviii)

1 Tbsp (15 mL) paprika

1 tsp (5 mL) coriander seeds

¼ tsp (1 mL) cumin seeds

¼ tsp (1 mL) fennel seeds

salt to taste

2 Tbsp (30 mL) tomato paste

6 plum tomatoes, chopped as small as possible

3–4 sundried tomato halves, roughly chopped

1 Tbsp (15 mL) muscovado or dark brown sugar

1½ cups (375 mL) water

1 14-oz (398-mL) can cannellini beans, drained and rinsed

4 Tbsp (60 mL) red wine

3 Tbsp (45 mL) balsamic vinegar

1 red bell pepper, cut lengthwise into strips and sautéed

3 bay leaves

1. In a deep nonstick pan, heat the oil for a minute or so over medium heat. Add the red and spring onions and cook, stirring, for 2–3 minutes, until soft.

2. Add the garlic and burgers (or other meat substitute), lower the heat and cook for 10 minutes, until the burgers are well cooked.

3. Sprinkle on the paprika and cook, flipping the burgers so that the paprika colors both sides.

4. Add the coriander, cumin and fennel seeds and salt. Stir for a minute or so, then spoon in the tomato paste. Mix for 1 minute, then add the fresh and sundried tomatoes. Stir well, cover and cook for 10 minutes, mixing occasionally to ensure that the mixture does not stick to the bottom of the pan.

5. Stir in the sugar, then add half the water. Simmer gently for another 10 minutes. Meanwhile, preheat the oven to 350°F (180°C).

6. Add the remaining water along with the beans, wine and vinegar, and simmer for 10 minutes.

7. Transfer the mixture to a lidded casserole dish and stir in the sautéed red pepper. Arrange the bay leaves on top, cover and bake for just under 1 hour.

8. Remove from the oven and serve hot over rice or baked potatoes.

BEAMING SUNSHINE RICE BALL

SERVES 4

THE CONCEPT OF BRIGHTENING UP OUR LIVES WITH VIBRANT, effervescent food inspired me to create this memorable dish—great for those gray days when you just know there's no chance of meeting the sun, yet you want to share something special with family or friends. This creation is a true work of art, and a great dish for kids. Best served with a simple green salad.

2 cups (500 mL) short-grain white or brown rice

6 cups (1.5 L) water

1 tsp (5 mL) turmeric

olive oil

1 medium onion, finely chopped

¼ zucchini, finely diced

1 cup (250 mL) vegan ground meat substitute, chopped roasted pecans or vegan burgers minced in the food processor

3 cloves garlic, finely chopped

salt to taste

2 tsp (10 mL) curry powder

2 tsp (10 mL) ground cardamom

6 dried apricots, chopped small

12 salted olives, finely chopped

zest of 1 lemon

1 cup (250 mL) canned or frozen corn (thawed)

1 carrot, grated

2 Tbsp (30 mL) diced red bell pepper

1 Tbsp (15 mL) egg replacer powder (see page xx), mixed with ¼ cup (60 mL) water

2 cups (500 mL) grated vegan cheese that melts—use either Vegan Mozzarella (see page 253), Mild Cheddar "Cheese" (see page 254) or purchased

3 Tbsp (45 mL) toasted breadcrumbs

2 medium carrots, thinly sliced lengthwise

1. Combine the rice, water and turmeric in a large covered saucepan and bring to a boil. Reduce the heat and simmer until the rice is cooked. Drain and rinse in cold water (to remove excess starch), then set aside.

2. Preheat the oven to 400°F (200°C) and grease a medium-sized casserole dish.

3. Meanwhile, heat the oil in a large nonstick frying pan set over medium heat. Sauté the onion and zucchini until transparent.

4. Add the vegan ground meat substitute and garlic, and stir.

5. Stir in the salt, spices and apricots. Cook over low heat for a minute or so.

6. Add the olives, lemon zest, corn, grated carrot and red pepper, and mix again.

7. Add the cooked rice, stir well and remove from the heat.

8. Finally, add the egg replacer mixture and the grated cheese. Stir well, so all the ingredients are evenly distributed.

9. Scoop the mixture into a large glass bowl, then invert it into the prepared casserole dish.

10. Sprinkle on the toasted breadcrumbs and bake in the preheated oven for 25–30 minutes, until it is crispy-looking. The inside should still be a little moist, making the textures interesting and contrasting.

11. Decorate with slices of carrot and serve.

MOUTHWATERING
MULTIGRAIN BAKE SERVES 4 GENEROUSLY

THIS RECIPE IS VERY ROUGHLY INSPIRED BY the traditional Maltese rice bake *ross il-forn* ("rice in the oven"). My version combines three grains—rice, millet and quinoa—baked together in a creamy, cheesy sauce. Millet, a highly nutritious, sunny yellow grain, is available in natural food stores. This is one of those dishes that tastes better the day after, so I always make a little extra. It's ideal accompanied by a freshly chopped salad.

olive oil

1 medium onion, finely chopped

2 cloves garlic, finely chopped

1 cup (250 mL) vegan ground meat substitute, hydrated TVP (see page xviii), chopped vegan burger or lightly toasted chopped pecans

1 6-oz (170-g) can tomato paste

⅓ tsp (1.5 mL) turmeric

1 tsp (5 mL) mild curry powder

7–8 cups (1.75–2 L) water

1 cup (250 mL) packed fresh spinach

salt and freshly ground black pepper to taste

2 cups (500 mL) uncooked long-grain white rice, rinsed thoroughly and drained (or brown rice, parboiled for 30 minutes, then drained and rinsed)

½ cup (125 mL) uncooked millet, rinsed thoroughly and drained

½ cup (125 mL) uncooked quinoa, rinsed thoroughly and drained

2 cups (500 mL) nondairy milk (see page 249 or use purchased)

2 cups (500 mL) grated vegan cheese— use either Vegan Mozzarella (see page 253), Mild Cheddar "Cheese" (see page 254) or purchased

1. Heat a drizzle of oil in a large nonstick frying pan set over medium heat. Fry the onion for a few minutes, until transparent and tender.

2. Add the garlic and stir for 30 seconds, then add the ground meat substitute and stir well.

3. Next, add the tomato paste, turmeric and curry powder, then add 1 cup (250 mL) of the water. Lower the heat and simmer the sauce gently for 20 minutes, stirring occasionally.

4. Add the spinach and the salt and pepper. Cook over low heat for another 10 minutes.

5. Meanwhile, preheat the oven to 400°F (200°C) and grease an 11- x 7-inch (2-L) casserole dish. Drop the uncooked grains into the casserole dish—this may appear odd, but go with it.

6. Add the sauce to the casserole dish.

7. Add the milk and cheese, mix everything well with a fork, then level it out with a spoon. Bake in the preheated oven for 25 minutes.

8. Remove from the oven and mix the ingredients again, adding 3 cups (750 mL) of the water (the grains will absorb some of it). Again, level the surface with a spoon, and place in the oven for another 25 minutes.

9. Repeat the same procedure as in step 8 (adding more water if the mixture looks too dry)—including cooking for another 25 minutes.

10. Since ovens vary so much, at this point you will have to judge when it's ready. Once the rice is soft, you're there. There should also be a crisp, golden crust on top.

11. Remove from the oven, and allow it to cool. I usually wait for it to cool completely before cutting all the portions, then heat them up again, and serve with a lovely salad and dressing.

SPICY RICE & QUINOA BAKE

SERVES 4

THE AROMA, TEXTURE AND COLOR of this dish are really quite astounding. Layers of spicy grains, luscious fried eggplant slices and a cheesy topping create a delightful one-dish meal that's sure to please. This recipe also works well with sliced mushrooms instead of eggplant. Serve with a salad of mixed lettuces, with a simple dressing of olive oil, apple cider vinegar and a drizzle of agave.

FILLING

1½ cups (375 mL) dry short-grain brown rice

6½ cups (1.625 L) water

½ cup (125 mL) quinoa

olive oil

1 medium eggplant, thinly sliced lengthwise (about ¼ inch/0.5 cm thick)

¼ tsp (1 mL) chili powder

¼ tsp (1 mL) coriander seeds

¼ tsp (1 mL) caraway seeds

½ tsp (2 mL) garlic granules

1 Tbsp (15 mL) tomato paste

⅔ lb (350 g) frozen spinach, thawed, or 1 lb (500 g) fresh spinach

zest of 1 lemon

12 spicy green olives, pitted and chopped (I use the salty ones with chili and garlic)

salt to taste

FILLING

1. Combine the rice and 5 cups (1.25 L) of the water in a saucepan. Bring to a boil, reduce the heat and simmer until the rice is cooked, 30–40 minutes. Drain, rinse and set aside.

2. Meanwhile, in a separate saucepan, combine the quinoa and the remaining 1½ cups (375 mL) of water. Bring to a boil, reduce the heat and simmer until cooked, about 20 minutes. Drain, rinse and set aside.

3. Heat a drizzle of olive oil in a large nonstick saucepan set over medium heat. Fry the eggplant slices on both sides until golden. Transfer to a paper towel–lined plate to absorb any excess grease, and set aside.

4. In the same saucepan, fry your spices in a little oil for a minute or two, stirring.

5. Add the garlic granules and tomato paste, and continue to stir.

6. Spoon in the cooked rice and quinoa, and mix well to enable both to pick up the flavors and aroma of the spices. Continue to cook, stirring, for a few more minutes.

7. Add the spinach and lemon zest, then lower the heat to minimum and to cook for another 5 minutes.

8. Add the chopped olives and salt, mix again for 1 minute and remove from the heat.

(continued next page)

SAUCE

1 cup (250 mL) nondairy milk (see page 249 or use purchased)

1 Tbsp (15 mL) cornstarch

1 Tbsp (15 mL) nutritional yeast

1 Tbsp (15 mL) grated vegan cheese (optional)—use either Vegan Mozzarella (see page 253), Mild Cheddar "Cheese" (see page 254) or purchased

½ tsp (2 mL) garlic granules

salt to taste

¼ cup (60 mL) sunflower seeds

paprika, for dusting

olive oil, for drizzling

SAUCE

1. Mix together all the sauce ingredients except the sunflower seeds, olive oil and paprika, in a bowl.

2. Pour the mixture into a small saucepan and heat gently, stirring constantly, until it has thickened into a rich, thick white sauce. Remove from the heat and set aside.

TO ASSEMBLE

1. Preheat the oven to 400°F (200°C). Lightly grease an 11- x 7-inch (2-L) casserole dish.

2. Place half the eggplant slices at the bottom of the dish.

3. Spoon in the spiced rice and quinoa mixture.

4. Cover with the rest of the eggplant slices.

5. Pour the sauce on top, and sprinkle on the sunflower seeds.

6. Dust the center with paprika, and drizzle on the olive oil.

7. Place in the preheated oven for 40 minutes, or until the top is golden.

8. Remove from the oven and allow to cool for at least 15 minutes before cutting into portions.

GREEN BEAN RISOTTO
in a Peppered Mushroom Sauce SERVES 4

THIS RECIPE OFFERS A DIFFERENT TAKE ON GREEN BEANS by making them the focal point of a risotto, accompanied by a sublime peppered mushroom sauce. I served this alongside my Juicy Burger & Potato Stew (see the recipe on page 152), and it was certainly a winner here at home.

RISOTTO

4 Tbsp (60 mL) extra virgin olive oil

3 cloves garlic, finely chopped

1½ cups (375 mL) arborio or other short-grain white rice, rinsed and drained

1½ cups (375 mL) water, plus extra as needed

3 tsp (15 mL) vegetable stock granules or powder

salt to taste

1¼ lb (625 g) green beans, rinsed, topped and tailed

PEPPERED MUSHROOM SAUCE

2 Tbsp (30 mL) olive oil, plus extra for drizzling

2 tsp (10 mL) vegan margarine

2 cloves garlic

2 cups (500 mL) fresh mushrooms, chopped

1 cup (250 mL) vegan cream (see page 249 or use purchased)

salt to taste

1 tsp (5 mL) crushed peppercorns

paprika, for sprinkling

RISOTTO

1. Heat the olive oil in a large, lidded frying pan set over medium heat. Fry the garlic for 30 seconds, stirring constantly so it doesn't stick or burn.

2. Add the rice and ½ cup (125 mL) of the water. Sprinkle on the vegetable stock granules and the salt, and mix.

3. Now add another ½ cup (125 mL) of water, and stir. Cover, lower the heat and simmer for 10 minutes, checking occasionally to make sure the rice isn't sticking to the bottom of the pan.

4. Add the remaining ½ cup (125 mL) of water, and stir in the green beans. Cover and simmer until they are cooked—if you need a little more water, add it.

SAUCE

1. Melt together the olive oil and margarine in a saucepan set over medium heat. Fry the garlic for 30 seconds.

2. Add the mushrooms, stir and cook until some of the juices reduce.

3. Add the cream and salt, and continue stirring until the sauce begins to thicken.

4. Turn off the heat, allow to cool, then process with a hand-held immersion blender.

5. Finally, add the crushed peppercorns.

6. Add the mushroom sauce to the risotto and mix well. Sprinkle on the paprika, drizzle with some olive oil and serve.

DROWNED PESTO DUMPLINGS
in a Rich Mushroom Sauce SERVES 4

THIS RECIPE TAKES ME BACK TO WHEN, AS A YOUNG GIRL, I shared dinner with my dear American friends, whose mothers' dumplings were always soooo good. This grown-up version, flavored with almonds and pesto and topped with creamy porcini mushroom sauce, is equally wondrous. It's great served with fresh corn, garlic bread and a green vegetable.

DUMPLINGS

a handful of fresh flat-leaf parsley, roughly chopped

1 Tbsp (15 mL) ground almonds

4 Tbsp (60 mL) unbleached all-purpose flour

1 Tbsp (15 mL) brown rice flour

salt to taste

1 tsp (5 mL) quick-rising yeast

1 cup (250 mL) grated vegan cheese—use Vegan Mozzarella (see page 253), Mild Cheddar "Cheese" (see page 254) or purchased

1 cup (250 mL) vegan ground meat substitute, hydrated TVP (see page xviii) or a finely chopped vegan burger

1½ Tbsp (22.5 mL) vegan pesto (see page 76 or use purchased)

3 Tbsp (45 mL) olive oil, plus extra for frying

MUSHROOM SAUCE

olive oil

1 large onion, finely chopped

2 carrots, chopped

2 cloves garlic, finely chopped

2 cups (500 mL) porcini mushrooms

1 small red bell pepper, roughly chopped

8 cherry tomatoes (optional)

1 cup (250 mL) mushroom or vegetable stock

1 tsp (5 mL) paprika

1 cup (250 mL) vegan cream (see page 249 or use purchased)

sea salt and freshly ground black pepper to taste

1 Tbsp (15 mL) fresh oregano or marjoram or 1 tsp (5 mL) dried, for garnish

DUMPLINGS

1. Process the parsley and nuts in your food processor until very fine crumbs form. Add the other dry ingredients and process for a few seconds. Add the cheese, ground meat substitute and the pesto, and process for a few more seconds.

2. Then, with the processor on low speed, add the olive oil in a slow stream until a ball of dough forms.

3. Remove the dough to a bowl and let it rest for 15 minutes.

4. On a floured surface, roll the dough into about 8 balls and dust them with some flour.

5. Heat a drizzle of oil in a nonstick frying pan set over medium heat. Fry the dumplings for a few minutes, until they're a little golden.

6. Remove the dumplings from the frying pan and set aside.

SAUCE

1. Heat a drizzle of olive oil in a nonstick saucepan set over medium heat. Add the onion and carrots, and fry until they get a little color.

2. Add the garlic, and stir everything around, watching that it doesn't burn.

3. Add the mushrooms and cook for 10 minutes or so.

4. Stir in the red pepper and cherry tomatoes (if using) and simmer gently, uncovered, for another 10 minutes.

5. Add a little vegetable stock to prevent sticking, then add a little more after a few minutes. Check that the carrots have begun to soften. If they haven't, add a little more stock, and simmer gently for a few minutes longer.

6. Once the carrot is soft, add the dumplings, and stir gently. Cover and cook for another couple of minutes.

7. Stir in the paprika and vegan cream and add the salt and a little pepper. Cover and cook for another 10 minutes.

8. Once the sauce has thickened slightly, it's ready to serve; if it's too thick, stir in a little more stock. Garnish with the oregano or marjoram and enjoy!

JUICY PORTOBELLO STEAKS

in a Peppered Cognac Sauce SERVES 4

THE TEXTURE OF THESE MUSHROOM "STEAKS" is satisfyingly juicy, and the flavor is second to none. It's an impressive dish to make, yet very easy, and a gourmet treat for anybody—be they vegans, vegetarians or omnivores. This also makes a great dish for a special occasion. Serve with fries or whatever else takes your fancy.

MUSHROOMS

vegan margarine

4 portobello or large oyster mushrooms, rinsed and dried with paper towel

FILLING

olive oil

1 tsp (5 mL) vegan margarine

¼ cup (60 mL) walnut halves

2 cloves garlic, finely chopped

1 cup (250 mL) vegan ground meat substitute or hydrated TVP (see page xviii)

1 Tbsp (15 mL) thick teriyaki sauce (see page 127 or use purchased)

PEPPERED COGNAC SAUCE

1 tsp (5 mL) vegan margarine

2 cloves garlic, finely chopped

1 cup (250 mL) vegan cream (see page 249 or use purchased)

2 tsp (10 mL) prepared English mustard or other hot mustard

1 tsp (5 mL) vegetable stock granules or powder

1 tsp (5 mL) crushed black peppercorns

1 tsp (5 mL) cognac

TO ASSEMBLE

1 red bell pepper finely chopped

finely chopped fresh flat-leaf parsley or basil, for garnish

MUSHROOMS

1. Preheat the oven to 400°F (200°C) and grease a casserole dish large enough to hold the mushrooms in 1 layer.

2. Heat a little margarine in a nonstick pan set over medium heat, and fry the portobello mushrooms for 2 minutes on each side. Remove them and transfer to the prepared dish.

FILLING

1. Using the same nonstick pan, heat a drizzle of oil and the margarine over medium heat.

2. Fry the walnuts, stirring for a couple of minutes, then add the garlic and continue to stir (be careful not to burn it).

3. Add the ground meat substitute and cook on a gentle heat, stirring, for 10 minutes.

4. Add the teriyaki sauce and continue to cook, stirring, for 1–2 minutes.

5. Using a large spoon, divide the mixture evenly on top of the mushrooms. Prepare the Peppered Cognac Sauce (see the recipe below).

SAUCE

1. Place the margarine and garlic in a nonstick pan set over medium heat, and stir for a minute or so.

2. Slowly add the cream and, as it starts to bubble, add the remaining ingredients.

3. Lower the heat and allow to simmer for 2 minutes before serving.

TO ASSEMBLE

1. Spoon half the Peppered Cognac Sauce onto the filled mushrooms, and bake in the preheated oven for 20 minutes. Heat the remaining sauce just before serving.

2. Remove the mushrooms from the oven and transfer to plates. Top with the remaining sauce and garnish with finely chopped red bell pepper and fresh parsley or basil.

EXOTIC STUFFED ARTICHOKES

SERVES 4

IF YOU LIKE ARTICHOKES, this dish will not disappoint. This is a Maltese-style recipe I have tweaked to perfect the flavor. I like to serve the artichokes on top of a simple salad of red kidney beans, black olives, garlic and parsley tossed with olive oil and lemon, for an impressive-looking platter that's a delight to taste and share.

4 fresh artichokes

juice of 4½ lemons, for baking artichokes and serving

3 cups (750 mL) crumbled white bread

6–7 sprigs fresh flat-leaf parsley

4 Tbsp (60 mL) roasted peanuts

4 large cloves garlic

5–6 sundried tomato halves, chopped

2 Tbsp (30 mL) olive oil, plus extra for drizzling

2 fresh red or green chilies

12 salted black olives, chopped

1 Tbsp (15 mL) vinegar

1. Thoroughly rinse the artichokes under the tap. Cut off the thick stems to the base of each artichoke, leaving a flat bottom so they can stand upright.

2. Fill a large bowl with water at room temperature, add juice of ½ a lemon. Soak the artichokes for about 10 minutes.

3. Meanwhile, place the bread in your food processor and pulse a few times. Add the remaining ingredients except the olives and remaining lemon juice one by one in the order listed, pulsing for a few moments with each addition, until everything is crumbled.

4. Remove the artichokes from their soaking water. Wrap one in a clean tea towel, then bang it against your work surface—this will help to open it up in readiness for stuffing. Watch out for the tips, as they are pretty sharp, but this stage is important, as you really need to be able to get into the centers to fill them properly. Repeat with remaining 3 artichokes.

5. Open the artichokes and stuff them with the bread mixture until full, getting as close to the center as possible. Add the olives on top of the stuffing.

6. Fill a large saucepan ⅓ full with water, add vinegar. Place the artichokes standing up in the saucepan and cover. Cook on low heat until the artichokes are softened—this will take anywhere from 30–50 minutes. Keep an eye on the saucepan and top up with water if necessary.

7. When the artichokes are done, sprinkle the fresh lemon juice on top and drizzle with olive oil. Serve on a salad of red kidney beans, if desired.

NOTE: **When you're buying fresh artichokes, check that they have a tight leaf formation and are fairly heavy. To test for freshness, press the leaves against each other—they should produce a squeaking sound. Extremely hard outer leaves that are opening or spreading out mean the artichoke is overmature.**

STUFFED TOMATO & ZUCCHINI CASSEROLE SERVES 4

THERE ARE SO MANY WAYS TO STUFF VEGETABLES. This recipe has a stuffing full of flavor, with vegetables that simply ooze their succulent, natural juices—a full-bodied dish suitable for any season.

RICE FILLING

1 cup (250 mL) long-grain brown or white rice

3 cups (750 mL) water

1 Tbsp (15 mL) olive oil

½ cup (125 mL) pecans, crushed

1 medium onion, finely chopped

5 cloves garlic, finely chopped

2 tsp (10 mL) curry powder

½ tsp (2 mL) coriander seeds

1 tsp (5 mL) nutritional yeast

½ tsp (2 mL) ground cardamom

salt to taste

extra olive oil

8 medium tomatoes

1 large zucchini

SAUCE

1 medium onion, quartered

4 cloves garlic, chopped

½ green bell pepper (optional)

reserved pulp from the tomatoes and zucchini

¾ tsp (4 mL) paprika (smoked, if you wish)

1 Tbsp (15 mL) extra virgin olive oil

salt to taste

1 tsp (5 mL) dried rosemary

1 tsp (5 mL) fennel seeds

FILLING

1. Combine the rice and water in a covered saucepan and bring to a boil. Reduce the heat and simmer until the rice is cooked, then drain, rinse and set aside.

2. Heat the olive oil in a large nonstick pan set over medium heat. Fry the pecans for a couple of minutes, stirring constantly to make sure they don't burn.

3. Add the onion, garlic, curry powder and coriander seeds, and cook until the onion becomes translucent, being careful not to burn the mixture.

4. Lower the heat and add the cooked rice, nutritional yeast, cardamom and salt. Stir until well blended, then allow to cool. Once cooled, the mixture is ready for stuffing.

5. Cut the tops off the tomatoes, and carefully scoop out their pulp, setting it aside in a bowl. Halve the zucchini lengthwise and scoop out the pulp, reserving also. Stuff the tomatoes and zucchini with the filling mixture, taking care not to split open the vegetables.

SAUCE

1. Process the onion, garlic and green pepper (if using) in the food processor for 30 seconds. Add the reserved pulp, paprika and olive oil, and process for another 30 seconds.

2. Add the salt, rosemary and fennel seeds and process again for a few moments.

TO ASSEMBLE

½ eggplant, diced

3–4 medium potatoes, peeled and diced into 2-inch (5-cm) pieces

½ cup (125 mL) vegetable stock or water

TO ASSEMBLE

1. Place the diced eggplant and potatoes around the edges of a large stovetop-proof casserole dish. Carefully sit the stuffed tomatoes and zucchini in the middle of the dish.

2. Pour the sauce over the potatoes and eggplant, but not over the tomatoes or zucchini.

3. Place the dish on the stove, cover and cook on low heat for 1½ hours, or until the potatoes are soft and everything is nicely cooked. Add the stock or water a little at a time as the sauce evaporates.

4. You may wish to finish this dish off by placing the casserole in a 400°F (200°C) oven for 20 minutes or so, until the tomatoes wrinkle and color slightly.

EGGPLANT PARCELS
in a Smoked Tomato Sauce SERVES 4

I LOVE MEDITERRANEAN FOOD with all its wonderful tomato and herb sauces, and I also love Moroccan tagines—the combination of these elements inspired this unique stuffed eggplant dish. Dried apricots give just the right touch of sweetness to the filling, complemented by pecans and spiced basmati rice, all baked in a smoked, herbed tomato sauce to add moisture and embellish the flavors. Serve the parcels with crunchy roast potatoes and a green salad.

EGGPLANT AND FILLING

9 dried apricots, halved and soaked for a
few hours

3 Tbsp (45 mL) extra virgin olive oil

1 large, firm eggplant (be sure the flesh
inside is white, not brown), sliced thinly
lengthwise

½ cup (125 mL) chopped pecans

1 small onion, finely chopped

3 cloves garlic, finely chopped

½ tsp (2 mL) curry powder

½ tsp (2 mL) turmeric

½ tsp (2 mL) ground cardamom

a pinch of chili powder, or more if you like
it hot

½ tsp (2 mL) ground cumin

1½ cups (375 mL) cooked white basmati
rice

salt and freshly ground black pepper to
taste

SMOKED TOMATO SAUCE

2–3 Tbsp (30–45 mL) extra virgin olive oil

2 cloves garlic, finely chopped

1 Tbsp (15 mL) tomato paste

1 tsp (5 mL) smoked paprika

½ cinnamon stick

1 14-oz (398-mL) can diced tomatoes

½ tsp (2 mL) dried oregano

1 tsp (5 mL) vegan margarine

½ tsp (2 mL) raw or turbinado sugar

salt to taste

EGGPLANT AND FILLING

1. Place the apricots (including soaking water) in a saucepan, adding more water as necessary to cover them completely. Simmer for about 15 minutes, making sure the pan doesn't dry up. Drain and set aside.

2. Heat a drizzle of the oil in a nonstick pan set over medium heat. Fry the eggplant slices 1 or 2 at a time until slightly browned on both sides, adding more oil as needed—a griddle pan gives them a lovely design. Remove to a plate and allow to cool.

3. Meanwhile, prepare the rice filling: heat a little more olive oil in the pan, and fry the chopped pecans for a minute or so.

4. Add the onion and garlic and cook, stirring, until the onion is translucent and the pecans begin to brown (that's when they give off their magical flavor).

5. Add the spices. Cook over low heat, mixing well, for about 10 minutes.

6. If the mixture is a little dry, do not hesitate to add a bit more oil.

7. Finally, add the rice and apricots, stir well and add the salt and pepper. Remove from the heat and allow the mixture to cool for a few minutes. In the meantime, prepare the Smoked Tomato Sauce (see the recipe below).

SAUCE

1. Heat the olive oil for a few moments in a nonstick frying pan set over medium–low heat.

2. Add the chopped garlic and stir for 1 minute, but don't allow it to brown.

3. Add the tomato paste, smoked paprika and cinnamon stick, mixing well for a minute or two.

4. Now add the remaining ingredients, cover and lower the heat. Simmer for 20 minutes or so, until the mixture is thick and aromatic.

5. Transfer the sauce to a casserole dish large enough to hold the eggplant parcels.

(continued next page)

TO ASSEMBLE

chopped fresh parsley or mint, for garnish (optional)

TO ASSEMBLE

1. Preheat the oven to 300°F (150°C).

2. Place 1 slice of the cooked eggplant on a chopping board, facing it lengthwise toward you.

3. Starting about ½ inch (1 cm) from the end closest to you and leaving ½ inch (1 cm) at the opposite end, spoon a portion of the rice mixture (about 2 tsp/10 mL, depending on the size of your slice) onto the eggplant.

4. Carefully roll the slice away from you until it is fully rolled and the stuffing is sealed inside. Ensure it is lying with the overlap upward and, if need be, stick a toothpick through the top for further security (you can remove it prior to serving).

5. Continue with the remaining slices—the technique should come easier to you the more you do.

6. When you have stuffed each eggplant slice, place them all in the casserole dish in a single layer, on top of the sauce.

7. Cover the dish with aluminum foil and bake in the preheated oven for about 30 minutes, removing the foil after 20 minutes.

8. Remove from the oven and garnish with parsley or mint, if desired.

BAKED STUFFED GREEN PEPPERS
with Sweet Potatoes SERVES 4

I USUALLY STUFF GREEN BELL PEPPERS WITH RICE as the main filling ingredient, but this time I thought I'd use millet instead—full of iron and vitamins, and with a very mellow flavor. This yummy stuffing plays up the bright yellow of the millet with corn, curry spices and crunchy nuts for contrast. And these stuffed peppers even come with their own side dish, baked with roasted sweet potatoes in a rich, red tomato-and-garlic sauce. Serve with crunchy garlic bread, and if you have any leftovers they heat up nicely the following day.

STUFFING

1 cup (250 mL) millet

3 cups (750 mL) water

4 large green bell peppers

olive oil

2 onions, very finely chopped

1 cup (250 mL) pecans or walnuts, finely chopped

3 cloves garlic, finely chopped

8 mushrooms, chopped

1½ tsp (7.5 mL) turmeric

2 tsp (10 mL) curry powder

2 tsp (10 mL) fennel seeds

2 fresh red or green chilies, finely chopped (optional)

1 12.3-oz (349-g) package firm silken tofu, crumbled

2 cups (500 mL) canned or frozen corn (thawed)

soy sauce

2 tsp (10 mL) nutritional yeast

2 Tbsp (30 mL) finely chopped fresh flat-leaf parsley

2–3 Tbsp (30–45 mL) water

STUFFING

1. Combine the millet and water in a saucepan, bring to a boil, cover and simmer for about 25 minutes, until it becomes fluffy (do not stir or it will become mushy). Drain and rinse, then set aside.

2. Next, prepare your peppers by slicing off the tops (about the first ½ inch/1 cm or so) and scooping out the seeds and membranes. Reserve the tops.

3. Heat a drizzle of olive oil in a nonstick saucepan set over medium heat. Fry the onions until translucent.

4. Add the nuts, garlic and mushrooms, and continue to stir for a minute or so.

5. Now stir in the turmeric, curry powder, fennel seeds and chilies (if using). Add the crumbled tofu.

6. Add the cooked millet to the mixture, and mix for a minute or so.

7. Finally, add the remaining ingredients (including the water, as needed). Allow the mixture to cool enough to handle.

8. Stuff the peppers using a teaspoon, then replace the tops. Stand the peppers up in a large casserole dish (you may need to use 2 dishes), making sure to leave space in the middle of the dish for the chopped sweet potatoes that are added during assembly. Set aside while you prepare the tomato sauce (see the recipe on the next page).

(continued next page)

TOMATO SAUCE

olive oil

6 cloves garlic, finely chopped

4 Tbsp (60 mL) tomato paste

1 28-oz (796-mL) can diced tomatoes

2 tsp (10 mL) vegan brown sugar

a dozen or so fresh basil leaves, chopped,
   or 2 tsp (10 mL) dried Italian herbs

TO ASSEMBLE

2 medium sweet potatoes

olive oil, for drizzling

salt to taste

SAUCE

1. Heat a drizzle of olive oil in a nonstick frying pan set over medium–low heat. Fry the garlic for a few moments, making sure it doesn't burn.

2. Stir in the tomato paste.

3. Lower the heat and cook, stirring, for 1 minute.

4. Add the remaining ingredients and simmer over low heat for about 20 minutes.

TO ASSEMBLE

1. Preheat the oven to 400°F (200°C).

2. Peel and chop the sweet potatoes into 2-inch (5-cm) pieces.

3. Pour the tomato sauce around the stuffed peppers in the casserole dish.

4. Place the sweet potatoes in the middle of the dish. Drizzle with olive oil and sprinkle with salt.

5. Cover the dish with aluminum foil and bake in the pre-heated oven for 1 hour.

6. Uncover the dish and bake for another 20 minutes, or until the sweet potatoes are soft.

LEMON SPICED DOLMATHES

SERVES 4

MY GREEK MOTHER MADE DELICIOUS DOLMATHES, or stuffed grape vine leaves—lemony with a touch of cinnamon. In this version, curry spices, lemon, rice and nuts come together to create an awesome dish. The lemony sauce complements the dolmathes wonderfully and brings them to the next level of juiciness and flavor. Serve hot with crispy roasted potatoes, or cold for a lunch or appetizer.

RICE FILLING

1 cup (250 mL) long-grain white rice

3 cups (750 mL) water

20–30 large grape leaves (see note)

½ cup (125 mL) sunflower seeds

½ cup (125 mL) raw almonds, chopped

3–4 Tbsp (45–60 mL) extra virgin olive oil, plus extra as needed

1 onion, finely chopped

4 cloves garlic, finely chopped

½ cup (125 mL) vegan ground meat substitute or hydrated TVP (see page xviii)

1 tsp (5 mL) curry powder

½ tsp (2 mL) turmeric

¼ tsp (1 mL) ground cinnamon

zest of 1 lemon

salt to taste

1 Tbsp (15 mL) fresh flat-leaf parsley

FILLING

1. Combine the rice and water in a saucepan and bring to a boil. Cover, reduce the heat and simmer until the rice is tender, then drain and set aside.

2. If you are using fresh grape leaves, wash them and boil them for 4 minutes or so. If you're using marinated leaves, rinse thoroughly under cold water to remove the brine and saltiness. Set aside.

3. Place the sunflower seeds and almonds in a nonstick frying pan set over medium heat and toast them for a few minutes, stirring every so often. Be careful not to burn them—you just want to bring out their flavors and give them some color. Set aside.

4. In a separate frying pan, heat the oil over medium heat. Fry the onion and garlic, stirring, making sure they don't burn. When they have turned light brown, add the vegan ground meat substitute or TVP and cook, stirring, for a couple of minutes.

5. Add the curry powder, turmeric and cinnamon. Give it a good stir, turn the heat down to low and allow the flavors to merge for 2–3 minutes, stirring occasionally.

6. Add the cooked rice to the mixture and stir well.

7. Stir in the almonds and sunflower seeds, as well as the lemon zest and salt. Mix well. You may need to add some more olive oil, as the mixture will be quite dry at this stage.

(continued next page)

LEMONY SAUCE

2 tsp (10 mL) cornstarch, mixed into a
  paste with a little water

juice of 1½ lemons

2 tsp (10 mL) agave or maple syrup

½ tsp (2 mL) curry powder

½ tsp (2 mL) turmeric

salt to taste

6 Tbsp (90 mL) extra virgin olive oil

¾ tsp (4 mL) garlic powder

a pinch of freshly ground black pepper

1½ cups (375 mL) vegetable stock

8. Remove from the heat and stir in the parsley. Transfer the mixture to a large bowl and allow to cool. Meanwhile, prepare the Lemony Sauce (see the recipe below).

SAUCE

1. Place the sauce ingredients in a bowl, mix with a whisk for a couple of minutes and set aside.

TO ASSEMBLE

1. Preheat the oven to 350°F (180°C) and prepare a large, lidded casserole dish for the grape leaves.

2. To stuff the leaves, open a leaf, lay it flat and place 1 tsp (5 mL) of stuffing in the center. Fold in the sides carefully and roll it up away from you. Then gently place in the dish. Continue to stuff all the leaves in the same way.

3. Pour the sauce overtop, cover with the lid and bake in the preheated oven for 30 minutes, until the leaves have tenderized.

4. Remove the lid and return to the oven for another 15 minutes.

5. Remove from the oven and allow to cool for 15 minutes, if serving hot. If serving cold, allow to fully cool, then refrigerate.

NOTE: You can buy grape vine leaves in jars, marinated in brine, in Greek and Middle Eastern grocery stores and in some supermarkets. If you can track down fresh grape leaves, boil them for a few minutes before using.

ROCK & ROLL SAVORY BAKLAVA

SERVES 4 GENEROUSLY

BAKLAVA, THE TRADITIONAL LAYERED PHYLLO PASTRY DISH found throughout Greece and the Middle East, is often served as a sweet, but this savory Indian-influenced version with nuts and spices is sublime. The phyllo layers give it a wonderfully crunchy texture, the filling is full of flavor, and the topping, a heavenly combination of agave, cinnamon and lemon zest, adds a note of subtle sweetness. It is truly awesome.
I like to serve it with garlicky sautéed mushrooms on the side.

---

olive oil

1 large white onion, finely chopped

4 cloves garlic, very finely chopped

¼ cup (60 mL) sunflower seeds

½ tsp (2 mL) turmeric

1 tsp (5 mL) crushed cardamom seeds or ground cardamom

1 cup (250 mL) walnuts, finely chopped in food processor

1 cup (250 mL) raw almonds, finely chopped in food processor

1 cup (250 mL) vegan ground meat substitute, hydrated TVP (see page xviii) or chopped vegan burger

1 Tbsp (15 mL) tomato paste

¼ cup (60 mL) water

4 oz (125 g) frozen spinach, thawed and chopped

salt to taste

½ cup (125 mL) chopped, pitted dates (stewed for 10 minutes in a little bit of water, so they're mushy)

½ lb (250 g) vegan phyllo pastry

1. Heat a drizzle of olive oil in a large nonstick frying pan set over medium heat. Fry the onion, garlic and sunflower seeds, stirring with a wooden spoon every 30 seconds or so, until the onion becomes transparent.

2. Add the spices and a little more olive oil. Stir well for a minute or so to combine, and enjoy the aroma.

3. Add the processed walnuts and almonds, and cook for 5 minutes, stirring every 30 seconds.

4. Add the vegan ground meat substitute, TVP or burger—you may need a little more oil, as the mixture will probably have absorbed it all. Stir thoroughly and cook for a few minutes.

5. Add the tomato paste and cook, stirring, for another couple of minutes.

6. Add the water, and when it has evaporated a little, lower the heat and add the thawed spinach and salt. Cook for another 5–10 minutes, then remove from the heat.

7. Add the dates and mix them in well. Allow the mixture to cool off a little.

8. Preheat the oven to 400°F (200°C) and grease a 9- x 13-inch (3.5-L) casserole dish.

9. Once your mixture has cooled, roll out the phyllo pastry into a circle about 6 inches (15 cm) in diameter. Spoon the filling

½ cup (125 mL) agave or maple syrup

½ tsp (2 mL) ground cinnamon

1 Tbsp (15 mL) lemon or lime zest

1 tsp (5 mL) vegan margarine

on top, starting about 1½ inches (4 cm) from the edge closest to you and making a horizontal line of filling about 3 inches (8 cm) wide. Leave about 1½ inches (4 cm) clear on the edge farthest from you, and about 1 inch (2.5 cm) on either side.

10. Roll the baklava away from you, until you have sealed the edge farthest from you. Now roll both ends inward and tuck them in.

11. Cut diagonal slits on top, about 2 inches (5 cm) apart, using a sharp knife. Then cut slits in the opposite direction to make a criss-cross pattern (see picture).

12. Finally, place in the prepared dish and bake in the pre-heated oven until golden—probably for just over 20 minutes, but as each oven varies, keep an eye on it to make sure it doesn't overbrown. Just before serving the baklava, prepare the Agave Sauce (see the recipe below).

13. Cut the baklava into slices about 1½ inches (4 cm) thick, and serve topped with the warm Agave Sauce.

SAUCE

1. Place all the ingredients in a small saucepan set over low heat. Heat, stirring frequently, for 2–3 minutes.

SWEET POTATO MOUSSAKA

SERVES 4

THIS VEGAN TAKE ON CLASSIC GREEK MOUSSAKA happens to be the best moussaka I've ever tasted. Sweet potato slices add a burst of flavor, layered with eggplant, a spiced tomato and pecan filling and a creamy white sauce. It's rich, delicious and impressive for a dinner party or potluck. Save time by preparing the ingredients ahead, and accompany with a simple green salad tossed with olive oil and fresh lemon juice, topped with black olives. This dish also works well the next day, when the flavors have had a chance to meld.

EGGPLANT AND SWEET POTATOES

olive oil

1 medium eggplant, cut lengthwise into slices ¼ inch (0.5 cm) thick

2 sweet potatoes, peeled and cut lengthwise into slices ¼ inch (0.5 cm) thick

EGGPLANT AND SWEET POTATOES

1. Heat a drizzle of the oil in a nonstick pan set over medium heat. Fry the eggplant slices individually until slightly browned on both sides, adding more olive oil as needed—a griddle pan gives them a lovely design. Set them aside on a plate in readiness for layering the moussaka.

2. Repeat with the sweet potato slices, setting them aside on a separate plate.

TOMATO SAUCE

4 Tbsp (60 mL) olive oil

2 large garlic scapes or 6 cloves garlic, finely chopped

1 medium red onion, finely chopped

1½ cups (375 mL) chopped pecans

1 large cinnamon stick, snapped in half

2 Tbsp (30 mL) dry TVP (see page xviii), hydrated in 2 Tbsp (30 mL) water

2 Tbsp (30 mL) tomato paste

3 cups (750 mL) chopped ripe tomatoes

salt to taste

1 tsp (5 mL) smoked paprika

½ tsp (2 mL) fennel seeds

1 tsp (5 mL) coriander seeds

2 tsp (10 mL) fresh marjoram or dried mixed Italian herbs

1 tsp (5 mL) vegan margarine

1 cup (250 mL) water

WHITE SAUCE

2 Tbsp (30 mL) unbleached all-purpose flour

2½ cups (625 mL) nondairy milk (see page 249 or use purchased)

¼ tsp (1 mL) ground nutmeg

salt to taste

½ cup (125 mL) Vegan Mozzarella cut into small pieces (see page 253 or use purchased)

1 tsp (5 mL) vegan margarine

1 Tbsp (15 mL) vegan cream cheese (I use French onion flavor)

TO ASSEMBLE

6 slices Vegan Mozzarella (see page 253 or use purchased)

extra virgin olive oil, for drizzling

paprika, for dusting

TOMATO SAUCE

1. Heat the olive oil in a large saucepan set over medium heat. Fry the garlic and onion for a minute or so, being careful not to let them burn.

2. Add the pecans and cinnamon stick, and continue to fry for a few minutes. Then add the hydrated TVP and tomato paste, and stir for a couple of minutes.

3. Stir in the remaining ingredients except the water, and lower the heat. Cover and cook for 20 minutes, stirring every few minutes.

4. Add the water and cook for another 15 minutes. Then set aside, and prepare the White Sauce (see the recipe below).

WHITE SAUCE

1. Place the flour and milk in a small saucepan set over medium–low heat. Whisk them together for a few minutes. Add the remaining ingredients and continue to whisk until you have a wonderful, thick white sauce.

TO ASSEMBLE

1. Preheat the oven to 400°F (200°C) and prepare an 11- x 7-inch (2-L) casserole dish.

2. Place a layer of eggplant in the dish, then ladle in about ⅓ of the tomato sauce, enough to cover.

3. Top with a layer of the sweet potatoes, followed by a layer of vegan cheese slices.

4. Add another ⅓ of the tomato sauce, then cover with about ⅔ of the white sauce.

5. Top with the remaining eggplant and sweet potato, another layer of cheese and the remaining tomato sauce. Finish by drizzling the remaining white sauce on top.

6. Bake in the preheated oven for 45 minutes to 1 hour, until the moussaka is golden brown on top.

7. Remove from the oven, drizzle with extra virgin olive oil and dust with paprika, then allow to stand for at least 20 minutes before cutting into portions.

VEGAN TAVA SERVES 4

TAVA is a traditional Greek Cypriot lamb recipe, named after the earthenware dish in which it is baked. Here is my vegan version, inspired by my Mediterranean lineage and the excellent cooking of my Greek Cypriot father. It's a succulent, rewarding one-dish meal, bursting with Greek flavors. Don't be put off by the number of ingredients—it's very easy to prepare, and not at all time-consuming, as the transformation happens in the oven. For a dinner party, serve with crunchy Mediterranean bread and hummus (see the recipe on page 25).

---

8 small vegan burgers (or equivalent quantity of vegan "beef" strips)

2 large red onions, roughly chopped

6 tomatoes, sliced medium thick

about 4 lb (2 kg) potatoes, peeled and chopped into 2-inch (5-cm) pieces

6 large cloves garlic, quartered

1½ tsp (7.5 mL) vegetable stock granules or powder mixed with 1 cup (250 mL) hot water

⅔ cup (160 mL) olive oil

juice of 1 lemon

1½ Tbsp (22.5 mL) vegan margarine

1 Tbsp (15 mL) agave or maple syrup

1½ tsp (7.5 mL) Dijon mustard

4–5 Tbsp (60–75 mL) finely chopped fresh flat-leaf parsley

2 tsp (10 mL) dried rosemary

2½ tsp (12.5 mL) cumin seeds

salt and crushed black peppercorns to taste

1 cinnamon stick, broken in pieces

1. Preheat the oven to 350°F (180°C).

2. Place the vegan burgers or "beef" strips in a 9- x 13-inch (3.5-L) casserole dish. Top with half the chopped onions, then half the tomato slices.

3. Distribute half the potatoes on top of the tomatoes, then top with the remaining onions, tomatoes and potatoes, plus the garlic.

4. In a bowl, combine the vegetable stock, oil, lemon juice, margarine, agave and mustard. Pour the mixture over the vegetables in the dish.

5. Sprinkle the parsley, rosemary, cumin seeds and salt and crushed peppercorns overtop, then the cinnamon pieces.

6. Cover the dish with aluminum foil and bake in the preheated oven for 1½–2 hours. After 1 hour, check if the potatoes are soft by sticking a sharp knife into them. When they are soft, remove the foil and spoon the juices from the bottom of the dish over the veggies. Add a little water if it's looking too dry, and return to the oven for the remainder of the cooking time, until the potatoes are nicely golden and crispy.

7. Remove the tava from the oven and serve immediately with a crunchy green salad and fresh Mediterranean bread, which is wonderful dipped into the juices.

GOLDEN FESTIVE LOAF SERVES 4

THIS IS ANOTHER IMPRESSIVE FESTIVE DISH that doesn't require endless time and effort. If you don't wish to be stuck in your kitchen for hours on end, but you do want to produce excellence at the table, this recipe is for you. It goes well with all the trimmings (I like rosemary roasted potatoes and small green peas) and it's filling, satisfying and childproof, too. The Peppered Cognac Sauce (see the recipe on page 168) is a wonderful accompaniment, but you can also substitute your favorite gravy.

1¼ cups (310 mL) short-grain brown rice

3 cups (750 mL) water

1 onion, roughly chopped

2–3 cloves garlic, roughly chopped

1 stalk celery

1 small eggplant, roughly chopped

2 Tbsp (30 mL) olive oil, plus extra as needed

1 tsp (5 mL) curry powder

1½ Tbsp (22.5 mL) tomato paste

½ tsp (2 mL) dried oregano

1 large carrot (make sure it's sweet and hard), grated

2 cups (500 mL) grated vegan cheese that melts—use either Vegan Mozzarella (see page 253), Mild Cheddar "Cheese" (see page 254) or purchased

1 Tbsp (15 mL) Nutty Parmesan (see page 262 or use purchased) or nutritional yeast (optional)

1 cup (250 mL) crushed roasted pecans

zest of 1 tangerine, clementine or mandarin orange, finely chopped

1 tsp (5 mL) garlic granules

salt to taste

2 tsp (10 mL) cornstarch or arrowroot powder, mixed into a paste with ¼ cup (60 mL) nondairy milk (see page 249 or use purchased)

1 tsp (5 mL) ground flaxseed

sesame seeds and toasted breadcrumbs

1. Combine the rice and water in a saucepan and bring to a boil. Reduce the heat, cover and simmer until the rice is tender—you don't want it al dente here. Drain and set aside.

2. Preheat the oven to 400°F (200°C) and grease a 9- x 5-inch (2-L) loaf pan.

3. Place the onion, garlic, celery and eggplant in the food processor, and process until finely chopped.

4. Heat the olive oil in a large nonstick pan set over medium heat. Fry the onion mixture for a few minutes, until it turns golden.

5. If the mixture seems dry, add a little more olive oil, then add the curry powder, tomato paste and oregano. Cook, stirring, for a few more minutes.

6. Meanwhile, place the cooked rice in a large bowl and stir in the grated carrot with a fork. Then stir in the onion mixture.

7. Stir in the grated cheese, Parmesan (if using), pecans, zest, garlic granules and salt. Add the cornstarch mixture and flaxseed, and stir well.

8. Spoon the mixture into the prepared loaf pan and flatten well with a spatula or fork.

9. Sprinkle the sesame seeds and breadcrumbs overtop and bake for 50 minutes, until golden.

10. Remove from the oven and allow the loaf to cool fully before refrigerating overnight, or for at least 3–4 hours.

11. Before serving, use a sharp knife to cut the loaf into slices ½ inch (1 cm) thick while still in the pan. Overlap the slices on a nonstick dish, then heat in the oven for 25 minutes, or microwave until hot. Serve topped with Peppered Cognac Sauce (see the recipe on page 169).

NOTE: If you can, make the loaf the day before you plan to serve it, as it will cut beautifully after it has had time to set properly. If not, make it at least a few hours ahead and refrigerate for a few hours after it has cooled.

MUSHROOM & WALNUT LOAF

SERVES 4 GENEROUSLY

THIS LOAF IS FULL OF GOODNESS, with a smooth texture and sublime flavor. I often serve it with a quick white sauce—made with almond milk, vegan cream and vegan cheese, seasoned with chopped parsley, garlic granules and salt, and thickened with cornstarch—but it's excellent on its own as well. The loaf takes a bit of time to prepare, but makes enough for leftovers the next day—although it's so delicious it's likely to get eaten up in one sitting by four hungry diners! Serve with a colorful side salad and crunchy roasted potatoes. It can also be served cold as a pâté.

2 cups (500 mL) short-grain brown rice

4 cups (1 L) water

1 Tbsp (15 mL) extra virgin olive oil

3 cups (750 mL) chopped mushrooms

1 Tbsp (15 mL) teriyaki sauce (see page 127 or use purchased)

1½ Tbsp (22.5 mL) unbleached all-purpose flour or tapioca flour

1 cup (250 mL) walnut halves, plus extra for garnish

2 slices of whole-grain bread (preferably a day or two old)

½ small red onion, chopped

2 cloves garlic, chopped

3 Tbsp (45 mL) fresh flat-leaf parsley

1 cup (250 mL) firm silken tofu

1 tsp (5 mL) garlic granules or powder

2 tsp (10 mL) ground flaxseed

2 tsp (10 mL) agave or maple syrup

salt to taste

1. Combine the rice and water in a saucepan and bring to a boil. Cover, reduce the heat and simmer until the rice is cooked, about 45–50 minutes. (Since cooking times for brown rice vary, do check it after about 30 minutes). Drain, rinse and set aside.

2. Meanwhile, heat the olive oil in a saucepan set over medium heat and fry the mushrooms.

3. When the mushrooms have softened, stir in the teriyaki sauce. Add the flour and stir until the juices have thickened. Remove from the heat and set aside.

4. Preheat the oven to 400°F (200°C) and thoroughly grease a 10- x 6-inch (3-L) loaf pan.

5. Process the walnuts in the food processor until chopped small, but not ground into a powder. Transfer them to a bowl and set aside.

6. Place the bread slices in the food processor, and process until medium-sized crumbs form. Remove and set aside.

7. Process the onion and garlic and set aside.

8. Process the parsley until finely chopped and set aside.

9. Finally, process the cooked rice, but only for about 5 seconds—you don't want it to be completely processed, just slightly. Remove and set aside.

10. Replace the food processor blade with the plastic pastry blade, then add the tofu. Process until fairly smooth, but not to a mayonnaise consistency—you want a thick consistency, like hummus.

11. Add all the processed ingredients back into the food processor, then add the remaining ingredients. Process until the ingredients are blended—a few seconds will do the job.

12. Transfer the mixture to the prepared loaf pan, decorate with walnuts and bake in the preheated oven for 30–40 minutes. Cut into slices and serve, with a sauce or gravy or on its own.

CORNISH-STYLE SAUSAGE PIE

SERVES 4

I WAS INSPIRED WHILE WATCHING THE DIFFERENT METHODS of making Cornish pasties in Cornwall, England, where many a person feels passionate about these wonderful pies (reminiscent of *pastizzi*, the traditional local snack here in Malta—see my recipe on page 40). This veganized version incorporates potatoes, green apple, veggie sausages and a twist of curry. The result is a succulent pasty to enjoy with a hot bowl of simple soup, or even a cup of tea. Ideal for the cold winter months, easy and not too time-consuming to prepare.

2 medium potatoes

1 large green apple, cored and sliced

½ tsp (2 mL) agave or maple syrup

olive oil

1 medium onion, finely chopped

2 cloves garlic, finely chopped

salt and freshly ground black pepper to taste

¼ cup (60 mL) vegan cream (see page 249 or use purchased)

1 tsp (5 mL) garlic powder (optional)

2 vegan sausages, cut into chunks

1 tsp (5 mL) curry powder

1 cup (250 mL) chopped vegan burger or ½ cup (125 mL) dry TVP (see page xviii) hydrated in ½ cup (125 mL) boiling water

10 oz (300 g) ready-made vegan puff pastry

5–6 oz (150–175 g) vegan cheese, cubed—use either Vegan Mozzarella (see page 253), Mild Cheddar "Cheese" (see page 254) or purchased

1. Peel the potatoes, place them in a saucepan and cover with water. Bring to a boil, cover the saucepan and simmer until cooked. Drain and allow the potatoes to cool, then cut into slices ¼ inch (0.5 cm) thick.

2. Meanwhile, place the apple slices in a medium saucepan with a little water and the agave or maple syrup. Simmer until soft, drain and set aside.

3. Heat a drizzle of oil in a nonstick pan set over medium heat. Fry the onion and garlic until transparent, stirring frequently.

4. Add the salt and pepper, the cream and the garlic powder (if using), and give it all a good stir before removing the sauce from the heat and setting aside.

5. In a separate frying pan set over medium heat, heat a drizzle of oil and fry the sausage chunks. When they're slightly browned, add the curry powder. Once the sausages are fully cooked, transfer to a bowl.

6. Heat another drizzle of oil in the same pan and fry the vegan burger pieces until they have some color. Set aside.

7. Preheat the oven to 400°F (200°C) and grease a nonstick baking sheet.

8. Prepare a completely clean surface for rolling out the pastry, and spread a thin layer of flour over it. Then roll your puff pastry into a circle about 10 inches (25 cm) in diameter.

9. Layer the potato slices in the middle of the pastry, leaving 1 inch (2.5 cm) clear at each end. Top with the apple, followed by the sausage pieces and burger pieces, and the thick white onion sauce. Finish with the cubes of cheese.

10. Close the pastry by folding one side over the filling, then folding the other side overtop the first, and tucking in the ends. Transfer to the prepared baking sheet and bake for about 30 minutes, until the pastry is golden and cooked.

11. Serve piping hot, cut into slices with a sharp knife—and catch a whiff of the wonderful aroma.

SHEPHERD'S PIE with Mapled Parsnips

SERVES 4

THIS DISH WILL FIT THE BILL BEAUTIFULLY for any festive meal or special Sunday dinner. It includes roast veggies and all the trimmings of a traditional roast dinner to make the centerpiece of a warming, hearty meal. Serve with carrots, broccoli and Brussels sprouts topped with a vegan cheese sauce, or with Zesty Cauliflower with Garlic & Basil (see the recipe on page 43).

FILLING

extra virgin olive oil

1 large red onion, finely chopped

1 zucchini, finely chopped

4 mushrooms, finely chopped

3 cloves garlic, finely chopped

3 cups (750 mL) vegan ground meat substitute or hydrated TVP (see page xviii)

2 Tbsp (30 mL) tomato paste

1 cup (250 mL) vegetable stock or mushroom stock

1 cup (250 mL) frozen small peas

1 tsp (5 mL) dried mixed herbs (sage, thyme, marjoram, oregano, parsley)

½ tsp (2 mL) cornstarch, mixed with ¼ cup (60 mL) water

TOPPING

2 lb (1 kg) potatoes, cut into quarters if small or 6–8 pieces if large

2 Tbsp (30 mL) vegan margarine

1 tsp (5 mL) salt

½ cup (125 mL) hot soymilk

olive oil, for drizzling

2 medium parsnips

TO ASSEMBLE

½ lb (250 g) sliced vegan cheese that melts—use either Vegan Mozzarella (see page 253), Mild Cheddar "Cheese" (see page 254) or purchased

a pinch of ground nutmeg, for dusting

maple syrup, for drizzling

FILLING

1. Heat the olive oil in a nonstick pan set over medium heat, then fry the onion until transparent.

2. Add the zucchini and mushrooms, and fry for a few minutes.

3. Add the garlic and continue to cook, stirring, for another couple of minutes, until all the ingredients soften.

4. Stir in the vegan ground meat substitute or TVP, then add the tomato paste and a little more olive oil. Cook for a few more minutes.

5. Add the stock, peas and herbs. Simmer for 30 minutes over low heat while you prepare the topping (see the recipe below).

6. Finally, add the cornstarch mixture and stir. You should be left with a thickish sauce. If it is too runny, allow to simmer a while longer, until some of the liquid evaporates. Then spread it out evenly in a casserole dish.

TOPPING

1. Place the potatoes in a saucepan and cover with water. Bring to a boil, then cover and simmer until very soft. Drain.

2. Mash the potatoes with the margarine and salt, slowly adding hot soymilk a little at a time. Mash until very smooth.

3. Steam the parsnips until slightly soft; slice lengthwise.

TO ASSEMBLE

1. Preheat the oven to 400°F (200°C).

2. Place the cheese slices on top of the filling in the dish. Then add the mashed potatoes, evening out with a spatula until smooth.

3. Place the parsnips around the edges of the dish. Dust ground nutmeg on top, and then drizzle some olive oil onto the parsnips, followed by a generous drizzling of maple syrup.

4. Bake for about 1 hour, until crispy and golden on top.

MINCE & ALE PIE SERVES 4 GENEROUSLY

FROM TIME TO TIME WE GET NOSTALGIC, especially in the winter, for English pies and country walks. That fresh, cold air penetrating one's being, then arriving back to the warmth of the home, with that smug feeling of having braced the elements, and the aroma of lunch in the oven wafting down the hall. This pie is every bit as good as the non-vegan version—better, in fact, as it's not packed with cholesterol. It's also easy to make. Serve with mashed potatoes and your favorite greens.

---

2 Tbsp (30 mL) extra virgin olive oil

1 large white onion, finely chopped

1 lb (500 g) vegan ground meat substitute

1 cup (250 mL) chopped porcini or other mushrooms

2 cloves garlic, very finely chopped, or 2 tsp (10 mL) fine garlic granules

2 Tbsp (30 mL) vegan Worcestershire sauce

1 Tbsp (15 mL) soy sauce

½ Tbsp (7.5 mL) tomato paste

1 Tbsp (15 mL) HP or other brown sauce

1 tsp (5 mL) vegan brown sugar or agave or maple syrup

1 tsp (5 mL) fresh parsley

½ tsp (2 mL) fresh thyme or ¼ tsp (1 mL) dried

¼ tsp (1 mL) freshly ground black pepper

salt to taste

1 11-oz (330-mL) can pale ale (substitute part water if you prefer it less strong)

2 tsp (10 mL) cornstarch, mixed into a paste with a little water

1 lb (500 g) vegan puff pastry or shortcrust (pie) pastry

1. Heat a drizzle of olive oil in a large nonstick pan set over medium heat. Fry the onion just until slightly golden, being careful not to burn it.

2. Add the vegan ground meat substitute and stir to combine. Lower the heat, add a little more olive oil and cook for 2–3 minutes. Add the mushrooms and cook for another 5–10 minutes, until they yield their juices.

3. Add the remaining ingredients except the ale, cornstarch and pastry. Stir and lower the heat.

4. After 10 minutes or so, mix in the ale and simmer gently for 15 minutes or so, until the mixture reduces a little.

5. Add the cornstarch paste and stir until mixture thickens. Taste for salt. Remove from heat and cool for 20 minutes.

6. Preheat the oven to 400°F (200°C) and grease a large, round ovenproof dish, about 10 inches (25 cm) in diameter and 3 inches (8 cm) deep or individual portion dishes.

7. Cut the pastry in two, with one piece slightly larger than the other. Roll the larger piece out on a clean, floured surface, until large enough to cover the dish base and sides. Shape it into the dish. Trim off any excess at the edges.

8. Pour the mince filling in the center and even it out with the back of a spoon. Roll out the other piece of pastry, place on top and decorate as you wish.

9. Bake in the preheated oven for 35 minutes, or until the pie turns golden.

THE PERFECT CHRISTMAS
ROAST SERVES 4

THIS FESTIVE GEM IS LOOSELY BASED on the traditional English Beef Wellington, a somewhat lavish and extravagant dish. So this recipe had to reach the same high standard of taste, texture and presentation—and it hits the mark on every level. It's much easier and faster to make than you may think, and it slices beautifully. The Express Crunchy Potatoes are a perfect complement. To round out the meal, serve with roast carrots or parsnips, greens and Peppered Cognac Sauce (see the recipe on page 168).

---

2 Tbsp (30 mL) olive oil

1 cup (250 mL) chopped onions

2 large portobello mushrooms, chopped

2 cloves garlic, chopped

1 cup (250 mL) crushed walnuts

1½ cups (375 mL) vegan ground meat substitute, processed vegan burger or hydrated TVP (see page xviii)

6 pitted dates, chopped

3–4 tsp (15–20 mL) agave or maple syrup or vegan dark brown sugar

2 tsp (10 mL) carob or unsweetened cocoa powder

1 tsp (5 mL) fine garlic granules

1 tsp (5 mL) fine sea salt

½ tsp (2 mL) Marmite (or other vegan yeast extract see page xxi)

¼ tsp (1 mL) ground cinnamon

just under ¼ tsp (1 mL) ground nutmeg

½ cup (125 mL) hot water

about 8 oz (250 g) vegan puff pastry

4 oz (125 g) Vegan Mozzarella, sliced (see page 253 or use purchased) (optional)

1. Heat the oil in a nonstick saucepan set over medium heat.

2. Add the onions and cook, stirring, for a minute or so. Add the mushrooms and cook for a few minutes, until they soften.

3. Add the garlic and the walnuts, stir for a minute or so, then add the vegan ground meat substitute, burger or TVP. Mix well, then cover and cook for a few minutes.

4. If the mixture is too dry, add a little olive oil or a tiny amount of water. Add the dates.

5. In a cup, combine the agave, carob powder, garlic granules, sea salt, yeast extract, cinnamon and nutmeg. Pour in the hot water and mix well with a teaspoon. Add this mixture to the saucepan, lower the heat and cook for 10 minutes.

6. Taste for seasonings and adjust if needed. Remove from the heat and leave to cool for about 30 minutes.

7. Preheat the oven to 400°F (200°C) and grease an 11- x 7-inch (2-L) casserole dish.

8. Once the mixture has cooled, dust a clean work surface with flour and roll out the pastry into a large circle, approximately 10 inches (25 cm) in diameter.

(continued next page)

1 Tbsp (15 mL) finely chopped fresh parsley

nondairy milk, for brushing (see page 249 or use purchased)

fresh or dried rosemary, for garnish

9. Spoon the filling into the center of the pastry, leaving a 1-inch (2.5-cm) margin around the edge. Top with the mozzarella slices (if using) and the parsley.

10. Roll up the pastry, starting at the side closest to you and rolling away from you. Continue to roll until the "loaf" seals itself. You may need to shape it a little, so that it resembles a loaf, before tucking in the ends or squeezing them together to close.

11. Using 2 large spatulas, carefully lift the loaf into the prepared dish. Then, using a sharp knife, score diagonal wedges in the loaf (see picture). Brush the loaf with some milk, sprinkle on some rosemary and place in the preheated oven for 30 minutes, or until it's golden.

12. Remove from the oven and allow to cool for 10 minutes before slicing and serving on warm plates. Serve with Express Crunchy Potatoes (see the recipe below), and pass around Peppered Cognac Sauce (see the recipe on page 168—it can be made a day ahead) in gravy boat at the table.

EXPRESS CRUNCHY POTATOES

2–3 large potatoes

1 Tbsp (15 mL) olive oil

1 tsp (5 mL) garlic salt

1 tsp (5 mL) dried rosemary

POTATOES

1. Place the potatoes in the microwave on high until softened—this usually takes about 15 minutes, but check them after 10 minutes. Alternatively, place the potatoes in a saucepan and cover with water; bring to a boil, reduce the heat and simmer for about 20–30 minutes, until a knife tip slides in easily.

2. Allow the potatoes to cool for a few minutes, then peel them with a sharp knife and chop each into about 6 chunks.

3. Heat the olive oil in a frying pan set over medium heat, and fry the potato chunks until golden.

4. Remove to a paper towel–lined plate and leave for a few minutes to absorb the excess oil, then place on a baking sheet.

5. Sprinkle on the garlic salt and rosemary, and place in the oven while the roast is cooking, for about 25–30 minutes. Before serving, for a magnificent presentation, remove the potatoes with tongs and place around the sides of the roast.

DESSERTS, CAKES & TREATS

RAW CHOCOLATE, FRUIT & NUT BALLS MAKES 25–30 BALLS

THESE BALLS ROCK AND ROLL—they are super-healthy, they taste divine and the texture is wonderful: soft and moist, with crunchy bits of nuts and a kick of lemon zest. But just try to stop eating them . . . They are so fast to prepare, and will disappear even faster.

1 cup (250 mL) pecans

½ cup (125 mL) pistachios

1 cup (250 mL) pitted prunes (the softer the better)

2½ Tbsp (37.5 mL) unsweetened coconut oil

2 Tbsp (30 mL) agave or maple syrup, plus extra as needed

1 Tbsp (15 mL) Kahlúa (optional)

zest of 1 lemon

½ cup (125 mL) unsweetened finely shredded coconut

3 Tbsp (45 mL) unsweetened cocoa powder

1. Place the pecans and pistachios in a food processor and process until they are very finely chopped, but not powdered. Remove to a clean bowl and set aside.

2. Pop the prunes into the processor and process until they are well broken down.

3. Add the coconut oil to the prunes and pulse a few times, until you have a soft but reasonably solid texture.

4. Add the remaining ingredients and pulse again. Taste for sweetness and add more syrup if you wish. Add the processed nuts and process for a few seconds.

5. Transfer the thick mixture into a bowl. Take a small amount and roll into a 1-inch (2.5-cm) ball between the palms of your hands. Repeat with the remaining mixture.

6. Place the balls in an airtight container and refrigerate for 4–5 hours before serving. They will keep in the fridge for up to 5 days.

CROSS MY HEART COOKIES

MAKES 1 LARGE AND 4 MEDIUM (OR 6 MEDIUM) COOKIES

THESE DELIGHTFUL HEART-SHAPED COOKIES—a marriage of maple syrup, pecans, dark chocolate and cinnamon—were intended as a Valentine's Day treat, but they're so good you'll want to make them every day of the year. They're even healthful enough to work as a breakfast cookie, if you're in a hurry (or just in the mood to eat cookies for breakfast!).

⅔ cup (160 mL) maple syrup

1 Tbsp (15 mL) vegetable oil

1 tsp (5 mL) vanilla extract

1½ cups (375 mL) unbleached all-purpose flour

1 Tbsp (15 mL) apple cider vinegar

a pinch of salt

½ tsp (2 mL) ground flaxseed

1 tsp (5 mL) baking powder

¾ cup (185 mL) chopped good-quality vegan dark chocolate

1 tsp (5 mL) ground cinnamon

⅔ cup (160 mL) roughly chopped pecans

2 Tbsp (30 mL) nondairy milk (see page 249 or use purchased)

1. Preheat the oven to 300°F (150°C) and grease a nonstick baking sheet.

2. Mix the maple syrup, oil and vanilla extract together in a food processor.

3. Continue to process, adding the flour half at a time.

4. Add the remaining ingredients and process for a couple of minutes, until you have a thick mixture.

5. Roll out the dough on a floured surface and use a cookie cutter to cut out heart shapes (you can make about 6 medium hearts, or 4 medium and shape 1 larger heart by hand). Place the hearts on the prepared pan, allowing a little space for expansion between them.

6. Bake for 12–14 minutes, keeping an eye on them so they don't burn. When ready, they should be a light brown, and a little on the firm side. They will harden further when they cool.

7. Remove from the oven and allow to cool for 10 minutes before transferring to a plate (or eat them warm!). Once they're completely cool, store in an airtight container.

INFAMOUS DATE & FIG BARS

MAKES ABOUT 8 BARS

WE LOVE DATES AND FIGS IN OUR FAMILY, so this twist on the classic date square is a definite winner. The combination of dates and figs sandwiched in a wonderful oat and vanilla crumble is an irresistible teatime treat with a cup of your favorite tea. Serve warm or cold, with vegan cream as a topping, if you like.

FILLING

1½ cups (375 mL) dried figs (the Turkish
    ones are best), stems removed

1¼ cups (310 mL) pitted dates

4 Tbsp (60 mL) warm water

2 Tbsp (30 mL) ground almonds
    (optional)

zest of 1 orange

juice of ½ lemon

1 Tbsp (15 mL) barley malt syrup

½ tsp (2 mL) ground anise

¼ tsp (1 mL) ground cinnamon

¼ tsp (1 mL) ground ginger

BASE AND CRUMBLE

2 cups (500 mL) rolled oats

1 cup (250 mL) unbleached all-purpose
    flour

1 tsp (5 mL) baking powder

a pinch of salt

1½ Tbsp (22.5 mL) turbinado or raw
    sugar

1 Tbsp (15 mL) vegan margarine

½ tsp (2 mL) ground cardamom

1 tsp (5 mL) vanilla extract

2 Tbsp (30 mL) date syrup

⅛–¼ cup (30–60 mL) water

FILLING

1. Place the figs and dates in a food processor, add the warm water and process until the mixture is a pulp.

2. Add the rest of the filling ingredients and blend again for a minute or so, until you have a smooth, thick paste. Remove to a bowl and set aside. (Wash the processor bowl at this point, as you will be using it again.)

BASE

1. Preheat the oven to 400°F (200°C) and grease a 9-inch (23-cm) round pan.

2. Place half the oats in a food processor and process for a minute or so, until they are ground almost to a powder.

3. Add the flour, baking powder and salt and process for a few seconds.

4. Add the sugar, margarine and cardamom and process again briefly.

5. Add the vanilla extract and date syrup and process again, adding the water a little at a time. The consistency should be between that of a crumble and a dough, making it flexible enough for both pressing down in the base of the pan, and crumbling overtop with your fingers. Should the consistency become too doughlike, add a little flour until it breaks down again.

6. Transfer the mixture to a bowl and stir in the remaining oats.

7. Take about ⅔ of the mixture, a handful at a time, and press it down as evenly as possible in the bottom of the prepared pan. The base should be about ½ inch (1 cm) deep.

8. Spread the filling on top and even it out with a knife.

9. Crumble the remaining mixture on top, and place in the hot oven for 25–35 minutes, until the surface is slightly browned.

10. Allow to cool before cutting into portions. Serve at room temperature, or heat each portion for 30 seconds and serve warm with vegan cream (see page 249 or use purchased).

MALTESE DATE & ANISE SQUARES

THIS RECIPE IS INSPIRED BY A TRADITIONAL MALTESE SWEET SNACK called *imqaret*. The original recipe is a deep-fried one—a date filling with a fatty batter—not very healthy, of course, but certainly not lacking in flavor. So, here is a healthier version that contains all the flavor, without the unnecessary fat. These are easy to make, and lovely with an old-fashioned cup of tea.

FILLING

3 cups (750 mL) pitted dates

½ cup (125 mL) water

1½ tsp (7.5 mL) ground anise or anise seeds

½ tsp (2 mL) ground cardamom

zest of 1 tangerine or a little lemon zest

a few drops of lemon juice

1 tsp (5 mL) baking powder

PASTRY

1 cup (250 mL) whole wheat flour

2 cups (500 mL) unbleached all-purpose flour

2 Tbsp (30 mL) vegan icing sugar

a pinch of salt

4 Tbsp (60 mL) vegan margarine

1 cup (250 mL) cold water

1 tsp (5 mL) vanilla extract

a few drops of nondairy milk, for brushing (see page 249 or use purchased)

FILLING

1. Place the pitted dates in a medium saucepan and add the remaining filling ingredients except the baking powder.

2. Cook over low heat for a few minutes, stirring occasionally, until the dates begin to get a little mushy.

3. Remove from the heat and add the baking powder. The mixture will bubble a little. Leave it to stand, covered, for a few minutes. Meanwhile, prepare the pastry.

PASTRY

1. Place the flours in the food processor with the icing sugar and salt, and process for a minute or so.

2. Add the margarine in 2 or 3 batches, continuing to process between each addition. Add the rest of the pastry ingredients one at a time, processing after each addition, until the mixture forms a ball.

3. Transfer the dough to a floured bowl. Put the cooked date filling in the processor and process for a few seconds, until you have a thick pulp.

TO ASSEMBLE

1. Preheat the oven to 350°F (180°C). Grease a 9- x 13-inch (23 x 33-cm) baking pan.

2. Divide the dough in half and lightly dust a clean work surface with flour.

3. Roll out the first piece of dough into a rectangular shape slightly larger than the base of the pan, to allow for shrinkage in the oven. Place it in the prepared pan.

4. Spoon the filling on top of the pastry base, evening out with a spatula.

5. Roll out the remaining dough, and place on top of the filling.

6. Brush the pastry with a few drops of milk, and bake in the preheated oven for 25 minutes, or until golden on top.

7. Remove from the oven and allow to cool. Then cut into 8 equal squares, and serve with a nice cup of tea.

BLOOD ORANGE & STRAWBERRY SORBET SERVES 4

THIS IS ONE OF THOSE MUST-TASTE-TO-BELIEVE TREATS, with a simple, healthful list of ingredients that produces an outstanding result. Delight in the flavors and texture, and enter the next dimension in frozen desserts.

---

juice of 4 blood oranges

14 large strawberries, blended to a pulp with a food processor or handheld immersion blender

3 Tbsp (45 mL) agave or maple syrup

juice of ½ lime

lime zest, for garnish

1. Combine all the ingredients except the lime zest in a bowl, and stir.

2. Slowly pour the ingredients into your ice-cream maker, and follow the manufacturer's directions for making a sorbet. Taste for sweetness and add more agave if you like.

3. Spoon into a plastic container with an airtight lid, and freeze. Or transfer straight from the ice-cream maker to dessert bowls, garnish with lime zest and enjoy!

NOTE: **You will need an ice-cream maker for this recipe.**

NUTTY ICE CREAM SERVES 4

I AM VERY PROUD OF THIS ICE CREAM, because it is just out of this world. It is packed with flavors—cinnamon, pistachio, almonds and cashews—which, blended together, make the nuttiest ice cream in the universe. The texture is delightful and smooth, and it's cholesterol-free and sugar-free. Try it, and you'll never look back.

1 cup (250 mL) each of cashews, pecans, and blanched almonds, presoaked for a few hours

¼ tsp (1 mL) ground cinnamon

4 cups (1 L) water

2½ Tbsp (37.5 mL) cornstarch

½ cup (125 mL) agave or maple syrup

a few drops of almond extract

crushed pistachios, for garnish (optional)

1. Place the soaked nuts, cinnamon and 1 cup (250 mL) of the water in your blender, and blend until the nuts are almost completely pulped.

2. Add the remaining 3 cups (750 mL) of water, 1 cup (250 mL) at a time, blending for 15–20 seconds after each addition. If you have a powerful blender with a sharp blade, you shouldn't need to strain the nut milk after blending, but if you find there are small bits of nut residue, pass the milk through a fine-mesh cloth or cheesecloth.

3. Combine the cornstarch with ½ cup (125 mL) of the nut milk to create a paste.

4. Combine the agave or maple syrup and almond extract with the remainder of the milk in a saucepan, and heat almost to the boiling point. Add the cornstarch paste, reduce the heat and simmer for 2 minutes, stirring continuously to avoid sticking. Your mixture should thicken nicely at this stage. Remove from the heat and allow to cool.

5. Transfer to a container and refrigerate for a few hours, or ideally overnight.

6. Make the ice cream in your ice-cream maker according to the manufacturer's instructions, and store in the freezer.

7. You may wish to decorate each portion with a few crushed pistachios when serving. Enjoy this heavenly nutty treat!

NOTE: **You will need an ice-cream maker for this recipe.**

CRÈME CARAMEL EXTRAORDINAIRE SERVES 4

I PRESENT TO YOU MY CRÈME CARAMEL. It compares very favorably with the non-vegan version—creamy, rich and full-flavored, this dessert will impress many a guest. It's easy to make, too. You can leave out the cognac if you're serving it to kids, though it adds an extra dimension of flavor. Serve this as chilled as you possibly can.

CARAMEL

4 Tbsp (60 mL) vegan white sugar or turbinado sugar

2 Tbsp (30 mL) water

CRÈME

1 12.3-oz (349-g) package firm silken tofu

1 Tbsp (15 mL) custard powder or cornstarch

1½ tsp (7.5 mL) vanilla extract

3 Tbsp (45 mL) agave or maple syrup

⅛ tsp (0.5 mL) turmeric

1 cup (250 mL) nondairy milk (see page 249 or use purchased)

1 Tbsp (15 mL) cognac

CARAMEL

1. Preheat the oven to 400°F (200°C). You will need either a glass pudding basin (about 6 inches/15 cm in diameter) or an 8-inch (20-cm) quiche pan or soufflé dish.

2. Place the sugar in a small saucepan set over medium heat, and warm until the sugar begins to melt around the edges of the saucepan—about 5 minutes. Shake the saucepan, then leave it alone until the sugar has completely melted.

3. Gently stir with a wooden spoon, and continue stirring over the heat until the sugar has turned into a dark brown, runny liquid—this will take another 10 minutes or so. Meanwhile, prepare the crème (see the recipe below)

4. Remove the saucepan from the heat and add the water, being careful not to let it splash you. If there are any lumps in the mixture, return the saucepan to low heat, stirring constantly, until the lumps have dissolved.

5. Remove from the heat and pour the caramelized sugar into your pudding dish. Working quickly before the liquid hardens, carefully coat the base and sides of the dish.

CRÈME

1. Combine the ingredients for the crème except the cognac, in a mixing bowl and blend with a handheld immersion blender until smooth.

2. Carefully pour the crème into the caramelized sugar–coated dish.

3. Bake in the preheated oven for about 1¼ hours, or until the crème turns golden. Check after 1 hour—if you insert a knife and it comes out clean, the pudding is ready.

4. Remove from the oven and allow to cool.

5. When completely cooled, drizzle a little cognac over the pudding and refrigerate, covered, for at least 3–4 hours.

6. Upturn the pudding basin onto a serving plate, then serve.

ROSY RICE & NUT PUDDING SERVES 4

MY DEEP LOVE OF EASTERN CUISINE is expressed in this heavenly, rose-colored rice pudding, delicately flavored with rosewater, cardamom and coconut. Brown rice won't work as well in this dessert, so indulge and use short-grain white rice, arborio or even sushi rice. It makes a great dessert for any special celebration.

¾ cup (185 mL) short-grain white rice, arborio rice or sushi rice

3 cups (750 mL) water

¾ cup (185 mL) mixed pistachio nuts and walnuts

3 or 4 drops natural red food coloring

2–3 Tbsp (30–45 mL) rosewater (see page xxi)

3 Tbsp (45 mL) water

2 Tbsp (30 mL) agave or maple syrup

¼ tsp (1 mL) crushed cardamom pods

1 Tbsp (15 mL) unsweetened coconut oil

1 Tbsp (15 mL) shredded unsweetened coconut

maple syrup, for drizzling (optional)

1. Combine the rice and water in a saucepan. Bring to a boil, then cover and simmer until soft—if in doubt, err on the overcooked side. Drain and set aside.

2. Process the pistachio nuts and walnuts in your food processor until finely chopped.

3. Place the cooked rice and food coloring in a large bowl, and mash with a fork, as though you are mashing potatoes (alternatively, you can use the plastic dough blade in your food processor). Ensure that the food coloring is evenly mixed in, then mash in the remaining ingredients except the maple syrup.

4. Pour some maple syrup into each ramekin dish, and place 1 tsp (5 mL) of the ground nuts in each dish.

5. Spoon about 4 Tbsp (30 mL) of the rice mixture into each dish, and level the tops with the back of a spoon.

6. Distribute the remaining nuts on top of each dessert.

7. Refrigerate for a few hours before serving. Drizzle with maple syrup if you wish, and enjoy.

NOTE: **You will need 4 ½-cup (125-mL) ramekin dishes for this recipe.**

ENGLISH SUMMER PUDDING

SERVES 4–6

WHEN WE LIVED IN ENGLAND SOME YEARS AGO, sunny days were so precious due to their rarity. Sometimes, when we yearned for the sun to come out but it didn't—well, I would try to bring the sun into our home. This summer pudding is a quintessentially English dessert, full of mid- to late summer berries. Easy to make, impressive at the dinner table and always to be served with lashings of vegan cream. This is quite a healthful dessert, as it uses whole-grain bread instead of white and agave or maple syrup instead of sugar.

1½ lb (750 g) fresh or frozen summer berries (any combination of red currants, black currants, strawberries, blueberries, blackberries and raspberries)

5 Tbsp (75 mL) agave or maple syrup, or to taste

4 Tbsp (60 mL) water

8 slices whole-grain bread, crusts removed, plus extra as needed

vegan cream (see page 249 or use purchased), for serving

1. Place the berries in a large saucepan, add the agave and water, and heat gently over low heat for about 10 minutes—not longer, as the berries should remain intact. Allow the mixture to cool.

2. Cut a slice of bread to fit the base of the bowl. Then dip 1 side of the bread in the berry juices, and place this slice face-down in the bowl, so that the "cleaner" side is facing up.

3. Dip all but 2 of the remaining bread slices in the berry juice in the same way and continue to line the bowl, overlapping each slice at the edges.

4. Spoon in half the fruit mixture using a large spoon, and place 1 of the 2 remaining slices of bread on top of it—there's no need to dip this slice in the juice. This helps ensure the pudding won't collapse when cutting and serving.

5. Add the remaining fruit and top with the last slice of bread. You may need to fill in any gaps with more bread, as you need the outer casing to be strong when you later upturn the bowl.

6. Place a saucer or small plate on top of the pudding: it should fit neatly inside the rim of the bowl, making contact with the pudding. Place a 3- to 4-lb (1.5- to 2-kg) weight on top before refrigerating overnight. Reserve any leftover berry juice, for serving.

7. Prior to serving, upturn the pudding onto a serving plate, and pour any remaining juice on top. Serve with a healthy dollop of vegan cream.

NOTE: **You need to make this pudding the day before you intend to serve it.**

NOTE: **You will need a 1½-pint (900-mL) glass pudding basin for this pudding.**

BOOZY CHRISTMAS PUDDING

MAKES ONE 2½-PINT (1.2-L) PUDDING

THIS MAGNIFICENT CHRISTMAS PUDDING WILL WARM THE HEART and get you fully into the Yuletide spirit of giving and sharing. A sweet marriage of dried fruits and nuts; rich, dark muscovado sugar; sherry and cognac; and Christmassy spices, it's wholesome, traditional and wonderfully cholesterol-free, too. You can serve this with hot dairy-free custard or vegan cream (see page 249), if you wish.

12 oz (375 g) black raisins

5 oz (150 g) sultana raisins

3½ oz (100 g) currants

3½ oz (100 g) dried cranberries

2 cups (500 mL) amontillado (medium-dry) sherry

4 Tbsp (60 mL) candied citrus peel

7 oz (200 g) ground almonds

3½ oz (100 g) chopped almonds

½ cup (125 mL) each whole wheat and unbleached all-purpose flour, mixed

½ tsp (2 mL) fine sea salt

½ tsp (2 mL) ground ginger

½ tsp (2 mL) ground nutmeg

1 tsp (5 mL) pumpkin pie spice or allspice

½ tsp (2 mL) ground anise

1 tsp (5 mL) baking powder

1 cup (250 mL) muscovado or dark brown sugar

4 Tbsp (60 mL) cognac

1 tsp (5 mL) dark molasses

1 cup (250 mL) whole wheat breadcrumbs

½ lb (250 g) vegetable suet (see note)

1 Tbsp (15 mL) sunflower or other light-tasting oil

zest and juice of 1 clementine or mandarin orange

zest and juice of 1 lemon

1½ Tbsp (22.5 mL) date syrup or molasses

1 cup (250 mL) nondairy milk nondairy milk (see page 249 or use purchased)

1. Combine the dried fruit and sherry in a glass bowl. Cover and let stand overnight—you may wish to stir it before you go to bed, to help ensure that all the sherry soaks into the fruit.

2. The following day, grease 1½ pint (900-mL) glass and set aside.

3. In a large mixing bowl, combine all the dry ingredients (including the citrus peel) and stir.

4. Add the soaked fruit and its liquid along with the remaining ingredients and mix well, until the mixture is soft and well blended. Taste for sweetness.

5. Spoon into the prepared basin.

6. Cover the bowl with parchment paper and tie with string around the lip of the bowl. Cover this with aluminum foil, and secure again by tying string around the lip of the bowl.

7. Place the pudding bowl in a saucepan large enough for you to lift it out easily, and add enough hot water to come halfway up the bowl. Cover and steam over a low heat for 4½ hours, checking periodically and topping up the water, if needed.

8. Upturn the pudding onto a plate and serve.

NOTE: **You will need to soak the dried fruit the night before making this pudding, so plan ahead.**

NOTE: **You can find vegetable suet online and in British food stores. Look for Atora or Community brands.**

CHOCOLATE, KAHLÚA & ORANGE TRIFLE SERVES 4

DEEP, RICH CHOCOLATE AND ORANGE ARE A GREAT COMBINATION. This trifle is not difficult to make—plus it's cholesterol-free, light and addictive. Look for vegan jelly powder online (see page xxii) or in natural food stores; if you can't find it, you can make your own by dissolving agar flakes in orange juice and nondairy milk, simmering for a few minutes then chilling until jelled (see "Agar flakes" on page xix for details).

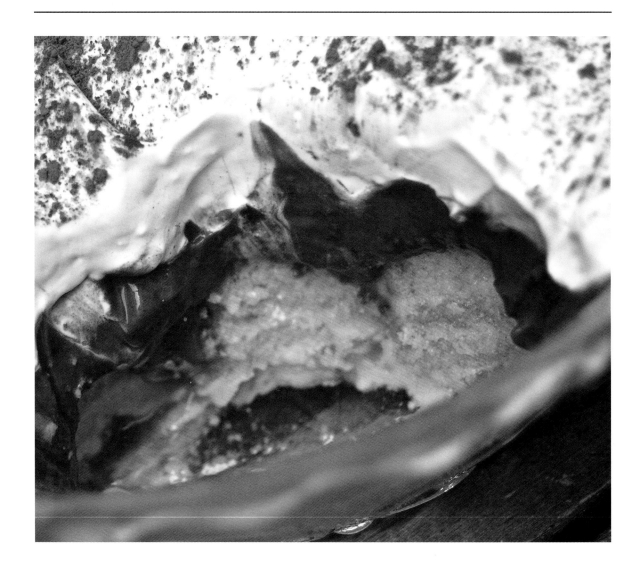

1 package vegan orange jelly powder

Happy Milk (see page 249) or other nondairy milk, for the jelly and custard

juice and zest of 1 orange

2 plain English muffins

1 tsp (5 mL) ground cinnamon

1¼ cups (310 mL) nondairy milk (see page 249 or use purchased)

¾ cup (185 mL) water

2½ Tbsp (37.5 mL) cornstarch

3 Tbsp (45 mL) unsweetened cocoa powder, plus extra for dusting

3 Tbsp (45 mL) agave or maple syrup

2–3 Tbsp (30–45 mL) Kahlúa

1 8-oz (225-g) tub plain vegan cream cheese

3 Tbsp (45 mL) vegan cream (see page 249 or use purchased)

maple syrup, to taste

1. Make the jelly according to the package instructions, substituting half the water with nondairy milk, then adding the juice of one freshly squeezed orange and topping up with water. Allow the jelly to cool for 15 minutes, then refrigerate for 1 hour, or until it sets.

2. Meanwhile, cut the muffins into slices ½ inch (1 cm) thick, and place them in the glass bowl. Place the jelly overtop. Sprinkle on the orange zest and dust with the cinnamon.

3. To make the chocolate custard, combine the 1¼ cups (310 mL) of the milk with the water.

4. In a bowl, mix the cornstarch and cocoa powder with about 2 Tbsp (30 mL) of the milk mixture.

5. Pour the remaining milk mixture into a saucepan and add the agave or maple syrup. Bring just to a boil, then pour it over the cocoa mixture, stirring well. Return to the saucepan and bring to a boil over gentle heat, stirring continuously. Then remove from the heat and allow to cool for 5 minutes, mixing occasionally to prevent a skin from forming.

6. Pour the Kahlúa overtop the jelly and muffins—but don't be tempted to add extra. Then pour the thick chocolate custard overtop, and allow to cool at room temperature for another 15 minutes.

7. Refrigerate for several hours, or preferably overnight.

8. Whisk together the vegan cream cheese, cream and maple syrup in a medium bowl. It should remain a little on the thick side. Gently spoon the cream cheese mixture over your set trifle, making sure you cover the entire surface.

9. Refrigerate for 1 hour, then dust some cocoa powder on top for decoration. Refrigerate for at least another hour before serving.

10. The trifle will keep well in the fridge for up to 3 days—though if my household is anything to go by, it won't last that long . . .

NOTE: **You will need a glass trifle bowl for this recipe, about 9 inches (23 cm) in diameter.**

HOT APPLE & CHOCOLATE CRUMBLE SERVES 4

WHAT DO YOU DO when you feel like eating two different desserts at the same time? I say, have them both. Tart, crisp green apples that infuse the air with their scent plus deep, dark, irresistible, hot melted chocolate, just waiting to ooze its aphrodisiac magic on the palate—a marriage nothing short of sublime.

APPLES

6 large green cooking apples, peeled, cored and cut into sixths

2 Tbsp (30 mL) turbinado or raw sugar

½ cup (125 mL) water

CRUMBLE

1 cup (250 mL) self-rising flour (see page xvii)

½ cup (125 mL) brown rice flour

a few drops of almond extract (optional)

2 Tbsp (30 mL) vegan margarine

2½ Tbsp (37.5 mL) turbinado or raw sugar

CHOCOLATE SAUCE

6 oz (175 g) vegan dark chocolate with nuts (the nuts are optional, though hazelnuts work well in this sauce)

1 tsp (5 mL) vegan margarine

1 cup (250 mL) vegan cream (see page 249 or use purchased)

APPLES

1. Preheat the oven to 400°F (200°C).

2. Combine the apples, sugar and water in a small saucepan set over low heat and stew until tender, about 25 minutes. Be careful not to overcook them—you don't want them mushy.

3. Place the apples in a 10-inch (25-cm) pie plate, and prepare the crumble.

CRUMBLE

1. Place all the ingredients in the food processor and process for 30 seconds, until a crumble has formed, with small pieces.

2. Sprinkle the crumble over the apples and bake in the preheated oven until golden, 20–30 minutes.

SAUCE

1. Melt the chocolate and margarine together using the double boiler method (see note).

2. Add the cream to the chocolate mixture, and stir gently until well blended.

3. Pour the chocolate sauce over the crumble, just out of the oven, and see you in heaven!

DOUBLE BOILER METHOD: **Pour 1 inch (2.5 cm) of hot water into a small saucepan set over low heat, then place an empty bowl over the saucepan to create a double boiler. Break the chocolate into pieces and place in the bowl. Allow the chocolate to melt completely, stirring regularly.**

RUBY RED STRAWBERRY CRUMBLE SERVES 4

THE JUICES THESE BERRIES YIELD when combined with maple syrup are simply glorious. Serve hot with vegan custard, or dollop on the vegan cream. In the summer, it also tastes out of this world with vanilla ice cream.

1½ lb (750 g) fresh strawberries, washed and sliced into 3–4 slices each

2 tsp (10 mL) turbinado or raw sugar

2 Tbsp (30 mL) maple syrup

1 cup (250 mL) unbleached all-purpose or whole wheat flour, or a combination

1½ Tbsp (22.5 mL) rolled oats

3 Tbsp (45 mL) vegan white sugar or turbinado sugar

3 Tbsp (45 mL) vegan margarine

½ tsp (2 mL) almond extract

1. Distribute the strawberries evenly in a 9- x 13-inch (3.5-L) greased casserole dish, then cover with the sugar and pour the maple syrup overtop.

2. Preheat the oven to 350°F (180°C).

3. Place the flour, oats and sugar in a food processor and process until crumbs are formed.

4. Add the margarine and almond extract and process for a few moments.

5. Tip the mixture into a large mixing bowl and continue to crumble by hand. You should be left with a crumble mixture, not a dough—if it overthickens, add a little more flour to dry it out.

6. Distribute the crumble as evenly as possible on top of the strawberry filling, cover in aluminum foil and bake for 20 minutes (baking covered helps the filling to cook and yield its nectar).

7. Uncover and cook for another 15 minutes, until the crumble turns golden. Serve hot.

LIME & COCONUT
CHEESECAKE SERVES 8–10

THIS IS A LIGHT, DELICIOUS DESSERT. Lime and coconut are such a fresh combination, and the kiwifruit decoration adds an exotic dimension and wonderful green color, and brings out the tartness of the lime. So this not only looks great; it tastes as good as it looks.

BASE

1½ cups (375 mL) walnut halves

½ cup (125 mL) granola

2 Tbsp (30 mL) vegan margarine

a drizzle of maple syrup

CREAM CHEESE FILLING

1 8-oz (225-g) tub plain vegan cream cheese

2 Tbsp (30 mL) agave or maple syrup

about 1 Tbsp (15 mL) fresh lime juice, or more to taste

BASE

1. Line the base of an 8-inch (20-cm) springform pan with a circle of parchment paper (this helps prevent scratching your pan when cutting).

2. Process the nuts and granola together in the food processor until they are reduced to crumbs. Set aside in a medium bowl.

3. Melt the margarine—you can do this in the microwave.

4. Pour the melted margarine onto the nut mixture and stir with a spoon. Then place a spoonful at a time into the springform pan and press the mixture down, evening it out with your hands.

5. Drizzle a small amount of maple syrup onto the nut base. Then place the dish in the freezer straight away.

FILLING

1. Place the cream cheese in a clean bowl, add the agave or maple syrup and, using an electric whisk, whisk very gently for 10 seconds.

2. Add half the lime juice and whisk very gently for another 10 seconds. Do not overprocess, otherwise it won't set. Taste to see if it's sweet enough—if not, add a little more agave.

3. Spoon the mixture into a bowl and refrigerate for a few minutes while you make the topping.

COCONUT TOPPING

1 14-oz (398-mL) can coconut milk, chilled in the fridge for a few hours or overnight

2 Tbsp (30 mL) vegan icing sugar

1 kiwifruit, sliced, for decoration

TOPPING

1. Ensure that the coconut milk is well chilled, and do not agitate the can—this is one of the most important factors in making this dish.

2. Set out a large bowl to catch drips below the coconut milk can when you open it.

3. Take the coconut milk out of the fridge and hold it over the bowl. Being careful to not shake the can, slightly open the lid. Then, squeezing the can enough to create a slight opening, drain out the water from the top. The idea is that you are left with the coconut cream only, which will be awesome by the time you finish—this will take a couple of minutes, so be patient.

4. Open the rest of the lid and spoon the thick concentrated "lump" of delicious coconut cream into a clean bowl. Add the icing sugar and, with a clean electric whisk, whisk it on a low setting for 15 seconds. Then spoon into a clean small bowl and pop it into the freezer for a few minutes (you can remove the cheesecake base from the freezer at this point).

5. Using a spatula, spread the lime cream cheese filling on top of the chilled base, making sure it is smoothed out evenly.

6. Take the coconut cream out of the freezer and use a spatula to smooth it over the cream cheese filling.

7. Decorate with the sliced kiwifruit as you please. Pop the cheesecake into the freezer for 1 hour, then remove, cover and refrigerate. It lasts for up to 2 days in the fridge, although it probably *won't* last that long—it's just too delicious!

BEST-EVER LEMON POPPY SEED CHEESECAKE SERVES 12

I ABSOLUTELY LOVE LEMON—the twist it creates on the taste buds is so mouthwatering. When it dances with sweet things, as it does in this creamy, rich and smooth cheesecake, it creates the perfect balance of flavors, making your taste buds sing. It's very easy to make and requires no baking. The kiwifruit decoration is a perfect flavor match for the lemon and its little seeds echo the poppy seeds in texture.

BASE

17 vegan digestive cookies, graham crackers or any plain, whole-grain vegan cookies

½ cup (125 mL) vegan margarine or unsweetened coconut oil, melted

½ cup (125 mL) walnuts

zest of 1 lemon

juice of ½ lemon

a pinch of salt

FILLING

1 12.3-oz (349-g) package firm silken tofu

1½ tsp (7.5 mL) poppy seeds

2 Tbsp (30 mL) agave or maple syrup

1 Tbsp (15 mL) vegan icing sugar

½ cup (125 mL) thin vegan cream (see page 249 or use purchased)

2½ Tbsp (37.5 mL) cornstarch

¾ cup (185 mL) water or nondairy milk (see page 249 or use purchased)

juice of 1 large lemon

sliced kiwifruit, for decoration

BASE

1. Grease an 8-inch (20-cm) springform pan and line the base with a circle of parchment paper

2. Break the digestive cookies into the food processor and process until crumbs are formed.

3. Add the melted margarine or coconut oil to the biscuit crumbs and process for 30 seconds.

4. Add the walnuts and process until finely chopped.

5. Add the lemon zest, lemon juice and salt, and process again for a few seconds.

6. Spoon the mixture into the lined pan and flatten evenly with your hands. Refrigerate for an hour or so, until cooled, while you prepare the filling.

FILLING

1. Place the tofu in the food processor with the poppy seeds, agave or maple syrup, icing sugar and cream. Process gently for a minute or so, until the ingredients are blended and smooth.

2. Make up a paste with the cornstarch, water or milk and the lemon juice. Place in a saucepan over low heat and stir until thick. Allow to cool for 10 minutes, then add the cornstarch paste to the tofu mixture in the food processor and process for a few seconds, until blended—don't overprocess.

3. Spread the lemon filling onto the chilled base with a spatula, and even out as best you can.

4. Decorate the top with the sliced kiwifruit.

5. Cover with aluminum foil and refrigerate overnight before serving.

CHOCOHOLICS CHEESECAKE

SERVES 8

OF ALL THE CHEESECAKES I HAVE TRIED AND TESTED, this is the one I created with chocoholics in mind. It's decadent, cholesterol-free and it rocks. Life with chocolate is divine!

BASE

13 vegan digestive cookies or graham crackers

2 Tbsp (30 mL) unsweetened cocoa powder

1 tsp (5 mL) instant coffee powder

1½ Tbsp (22.5 mL) vegan icing sugar

½ cup (125 mL) walnuts

½ cup (125 mL) vegan margarine or unsweetened coconut oil, melted

zest of 1 orange or tangerine

a pinch of salt

2 Tbsp (30 mL) Kahlúa

FILLING

4 oz (125 g) dark chocolate

3 Tbsp (45 mL) unsweetened cocoa powder

3½ Tbsp (52.5 mL) hot water

1 12.3-oz (349-g) package firm silken tofu

2 Tbsp (30 mL) agave or maple syrup

1 Tbsp (15 mL) vegan icing sugar

shavings of dark chocolate, for decoration

BASE

1. Grease an 8-inch (20-cm) springform pan and line the bottom with parchment paper.

2. Break the digestive cookies into a food processor and process until crumbs are formed.

3. Add the cocoa powder, coffee powder and icing sugar. Pulse for a few seconds.

4. Add the walnuts and process for just a few moments—you don't want them powdered.

5. Add the melted margarine or coconut oil and process for 30 seconds.

6. Add the zest, salt and Kahlúa, and process again for a few seconds. Spoon the mixture into the lined pan and flatten evenly with your hands. Refrigerate for an hour or so, until cooled, while you prepare the filling.

FILLING

1. Melt the dark chocolate, either in the microwave or using the double boiler method (see page 225).

2. Meanwhile, in a small bowl, mix the cocoa powder into a paste with the hot water. Allow to cool for a few minutes.

3. Place the tofu in the food processor with the melted chocolate, cocoa paste, agave or maple syrup and sugar. Process gently for a minute or so, until the ingredients are well blended and smooth.

4. Spread the filling onto the chilled base with a spatula and even out as best you can. Decorate with shavings of dark chocolate.

5. Cover with aluminum foil and refrigerate overnight before serving.

PINEAPPLE & PRUNE UPSIDE-DOWN SPONGE SERVES 4

THIS IS SUCH A SIMPLE, YET YUMMY CONCEPT—prunes and pineapple in a moist upside-down sponge cake. Food for the heart and a light dessert to round off a dinner menu. It's also a healthy treat for the kids. This works well served with Happy Cream (see the recipe on page 249).

---

1 14-oz (398-mL) can pineapple rings, drained

8 pitted prunes

1¾ cups (435 mL) unbleached all-purpose flour

4 Tbsp (60 mL) soy flour

1 Tbsp (15 mL) baking powder

4 Tbsp (60 mL) sunflower or other light-tasting vegetable oil

6 Tbsp (90 mL) vegan brown sugar

1. Preheat the oven to 350°F (180°C) and grease a Pyrex bowl 5 inches (12 cm) in diameter with vegetable oil or vegan margarine.

2. Prepare your fruit by reserving 4 or 5 pineapple rings for decoration, and cutting the remaining pineapple rings in quarters and the prunes in half. Set aside.

3. To make the cake mixture, combine the flours and baking powder in a mixing bowl.

4. Add the oil, mixing vigorously to ensure that you get air into the mixture.

5. Now add the brown sugar, continuing to mix.

6. Check that the mixture has the right consistency—it should be thick enough that it slowly drops from your spoon. If not, mix in a little water until you get the desired consistency.

7. Add the fruit to the cake mixture, ensuring it is evenly distributed.

8. Line the Pyrex bowl with the whole pineapple rings, and place a prune half in the center of each. Spoon the mixture into the prepared bowl and bake in the preheated oven for 30–40 minutes. Remove and check if the cake is cooked by inserting a sharp knife or skewer into the center. If it comes out clean, the cake is ready.

9. Remove from the oven and turn upside down onto a serving plate.

DOUBLE CHOCOLATE COKE CAKE SERVES 6

THIS DELIGHT REFLECTS MY VERY OCCASIONAL CRAVING for cola and chocolate—
I married the two and came up with a cake that is divine in all ways possible, with a frosting
that is simply luscious. The cola flavor does not overpower, but complements the chocolate
perfectly. Look for a natural brand of cola, with no artificial colors or additives (I use Fentimans
Curiosity Cola), and adjust the amount of sugar to suit your taste.

CAKE

2¼ cups (560 mL) unbleached self-rising
   flour (see page xvii)

¾ cup (185 mL) muscovado or dark
   brown sugar

¼ cup (60 mL) unsweetened cocoa
   powder

1 tsp (5 mL) baking soda

1 tsp (5 mL) egg replacer powder
   (see page xx)

¾ cup (185 mL) canola oil

¾ cup (185 mL) nondairy milk (see page
   249 or use purchased)

1 tsp (5 mL) vanilla extract

¾ cup (185 mL) cola

1 Tbsp (15 mL) apple cider vinegar

FROSTING

1 cup (250 mL) unsweetened cocoa
   powder, plus extra as needed, dissolved
   in a little hot water

1 Tbsp (15 mL) instant coffee powder

1 8-oz (225-g) tub plain vegan cream
   cheese

1 Tbsp (15 mL) cola

1½ cups (375 mL) vegan icing sugar

CAKE

1. Preheat the oven to 350°F (180°C). Grease a 9- x 5-inch (2-L)
loaf pan and line the bottom with parchment paper. Lightly grease
the parchment paper.

2. Sift all the dry ingredients together into a large bowl, then
sift again into another large bowl.

3. Add the liquid ingredients one at a time, mixing well with a
wooden spoon after each addition. Continue mixing for a couple
of minutes, and then pour into the prepared loaf pan.

4. Bake for about 45 minutes, or until a skewer or sharp knife
inserted in the center comes out clean.

5. Allow the cake to cool, then remove from the pan and
transfer to a cake stand or plate.

FROSTING

1. Whisk all the frosting ingredients together in a medium bowl
until very smooth, adding more cocoa powder if the frosting is
not thick enough, or a little water if it's too thick.

2. Refrigerate for 1 hour.

(continued next page)

TO ASSEMBLE

vegan dark chocolate shavings, for decoration

TO ASSEMBLE

1. When the cake has completely cooled, use a long serrated knife to slice it horizontally about 1 inch (2.5 cm) from the base, and spread some frosting on the base layer. Place the remainder of the cake on top, then repeat the process, slicing and layering with frosting at 1-inch (2.5-cm) intervals, until you reach the top of the cake. Cut off any bumpy, hard or uneven bits on the top layer, if you like. Cover the top of the cake with frosting, finishing off with the sides.

2. Garnish with some dark chocolate shavings. Refrigerate for 1 hour, covered if possible, before serving.

NOTE: I use a 9- x 5-inch (2-L) loaf pan for a different shape—however, the consistency is that of a normal moist chocolate cake. If you prefer, you can use a regular cake pan.

LUSCIOUS RED VELVET CAKE

IF YOU'RE A CHOCOLATE LOVER, you will love this moister-than-moist, full-of-flavor, light-textured red velvet cake. The rich, mouthwatering chocolate frosting, with a secret ingredient (strawberry or black currant jam), is the best I have concocted to date. Plus, it's very easy to make. I hope you enjoy this cake as much as my family does.

CAKE

- 3 cups (750 mL) unbleached all-purpose flour
- 1¾ cups (435 mL) vegan brown sugar (muscovado is great)
- 2 tsp (10 mL) baking soda
- ¾ cup (185 mL) unsweetened cocoa powder
- 1 tsp (5 mL) fine sea salt
- ¾ cup (185 mL) canola oil
- 2 Tbsp (30 mL) apple cider vinegar
- 1 Tbsp (15 mL) vanilla extract
- a few drops of natural red food coloring
- 1¾ cups (435 mL) cold water

CAKE

1. Preheat the oven to 375°F (190°C). Line the bottom of an 8-inch (20-cm) round pan with a circle of parchment paper, then grease the paper (to prevent the cake from sticking, which it is inclined to do).

2. Gather all the cake ingredients on your work surface.

3. Combine all the dry ingredients in a large mixing bowl and lightly stir them.

4. Add the wet ingredients one at a time in the order listed stirring after each addition. Continue to mix well with a wooden spoon until smooth and thick, but don't overmix.

5. Transfer the batter to the prepared pan and bake for about 50 minutes. Be careful not to overbake. The cake is ready when a skewer or sharp knife inserted in the center comes out clean.

6. Allow the cake to cool completely. Meanwhile, make the frosting.

(continued next page)

FROSTING

5 oz (150 g) good-quality vegan dark
    chocolate

5 Tbsp (75 mL) vegan margarine,
    softened

1½ Tbsp (22.5 mL) unsweetened cocoa
    powder

4 Tbsp (60 mL) vegan icing sugar

a pinch of salt

2 Tbsp (30 mL) strawberry or black
    currant jam

FROSTING

1. Melt the chocolate using the double boiler method (see page 225) or in the microwave.

2. Meanwhile, using a small whisk, whip the margarine and cocoa together in a medium bowl. Add the icing sugar a little at a time, whisking, so that you have a nice, thick cream consistency.

3. Add the salt and jam, and continue to mix.

4. When the chocolate is melted, add it to the rest of the frosting mixture, and mix well until it is velvety, creamy and smooth.

5. Refrigerate the frosting for 30 minutes (or see step 7).

6. When the cake has cooled, invert it onto a plate, remove the parchment paper and invert it again onto a serving plate. Apply the frosting to the cake with a spatula.

7. Alternately, if you want the frosting to have a slightly looser consistency, frost the cake before it has cooled completely and with the frosting at room temperature.

8. Refrigerate the cake after either method of frosting.

NOTE: **Don't be tempted to use whole-grain flour for this recipe, as the cake will not come out as moist, fluffy or light—unbleached all-purpose flour works best.**

NUTAHOLICS CHOCOLATE BARS MAKES 10–12 BARS

INTRODUCING ONE OF THE BEST BARS EVER CREATED, and probably the nuttiest—featuring almonds, pistachios, peanuts, Brazil nuts and coconut. These will satisfy any Snickers bar cravings, but they're far richer and more refined in taste, not to mention much healthier. A little of these bars goes a long way—cut them into small pieces to serve at a party, or wrap them up for a snack on the go. They also make a lovely gift, packaged in a pretty cookie tin.

(continued next page)

NUT LAYER

1 cup (250 mL) pitted dates and prunes, mixed

½ cup (125 mL) Brazil nuts

⅓ cup (80 mL) roasted salted peanuts

½ cup (125 mL) shredded unsweetened coconut

1 tsp (5 mL) salt

⅓ cup (80 mL) pistachios

1 Tbsp (15 mL) unsweetened coconut oil

1½ Tbsp (22.5 mL) unsweetened cocoa powder

2 Tbsp (30 mL) maple syrup

PEANUT BUTTER LAYER

1 cup (250 mL) peanut butter

½ cup (125 mL) raw almonds, roughly chopped

CHOCOLATE LAYER

7 oz (200 g) good-quality vegan dark chocolate

1 Tbsp (15 mL) unsweetened coconut oil

NUT LAYER

1. Process the dates and prunes together in your food processor until smooth.

2. Add the rest of the ingredients one at a time, pulsing between each addition—you want the nuts to break down, but not be too finely ground. Set aside.

CHOCOLATE LAYER

1. Place the dark chocolate and coconut oil in a bowl and microwave until melted, or melt using the double boiler method (see page 225).

TO ASSEMBLE

1. Line the base of an airtight plastic container, about 5 x 8 inches (12 x 20-cm), with parchment paper.

2. Pour half the melted chocolate mixture into the container and place in the freezer for 20 minutes, or until solid.

3. Remove from the freezer and place the nut layer mixture evenly on top, using the back of a spoon to level it out. Place in the freezer again for 15 minutes or so.

4. Spread the peanut butter on top of the nut layer, again smoothing it out evenly with the back of a spoon. Sprinkle the raw almond pieces on top.

5. Pour on the remaining melted chocolate, then agitate the container to ensure even spreading of the chocolate. Place in the freezer for 20 minutes.

6. Remove from the freezer, cover and refrigerate for 1 hour before cutting into bars.

BOUNTIFUL COCONUT CHOCOLATE BARS

MAKES 4–6 LARGE BARS

IF YOU LOVE COCONUT and have fond memories of Bounty chocolate bars, as I do, these bars are for you. They may look a little more rustic than the factory-made version, but the taste is far better, and they're far healthier, too. With a moist coconut center and a wonderful chocolate coating, these bars are addictive—consider yourself warned.

7 oz (200 g) good-quality vegan dark chocolate

1 heaped tsp (7 mL) unsweetened coconut oil

a pinch of salt

1½ Tbsp (22.5 mL) unsweetened coconut oil

1½ cups (375 mL) unsweetened finely shredded coconut

1 Tbsp (15 mL) vegan white sugar

4 Tbsp (60 mL) water

1. Line a rectangular plastic container, about 4 x 5½ inches (10 x 14-cm), with parchment paper and set aside.

2. Place the chocolate, the heaped tsp (7 mL) of coconut oil and the salt in a glass bowl and microwave on high for about 1 minute, until melted, or melt using the double boiler method (see page 225).

3. Place the 1½ Tbsp (22.5 mL) of coconut oil in a small saucepan and heat gently until melted. Add the shredded coconut, sugar and water. Stir for a couple of minutes over low heat, then remove and set aside to cool.

4. Pour a few spoonfuls of the melted chocolate in the pre-pared container. Place in the freezer for 20 minutes or so, until the chocolate solidifies.

5. Remove from the freezer and spoon the coconut filling on top of the chocolate base. Place in the freezer for a further 15 minutes.

6. Remove from the freezer and pour the remaining chocolate on top of the coconut filling. Place in the freezer again for 20 minutes, until solid but not frozen.

7. Remove the container from the freezer and turn upside down, releasing the bar. Remove the parchment paper and cut into smaller bars or other desired shapes. Store in an airtight container for up to 1 week.

AFTER LATE DINNER MINTS

MAKES ABOUT ONE 7-INCH (18-CM) SQUARE

I'VE ALWAYS LOVED THE IDEA OF A MINIATURE AFTER-DINNER SWEET as an elegant way to finish off a well-rounded meal. And if it has the digestive qualities of mint, even better. The problem lies in self-restraint—something this little delicacy challenges on a large scale. Suffice it to say, by the time the coffee is topped up, a scraping of chocolate and a whiff of mint will be all that remain on the serving plate.

COATING

4 oz (125 g) good-quality vegan dark
chocolate

2 tsp (10 mL) vegan margarine or
unsweetened coconut oil

a few drops of peppermint oil

3 fresh mint leaves, very finely chopped

FILLING

2 tsp (10 mL) cornstarch

2 tsp (10 mL) vegan icing sugar

3 Tbsp (45 mL) unsweetened coconut oil

1 tsp (5 mL) peppermint extract

1 Tbsp (15 mL) nondairy milk (see page
249 or use purchased)

3 fresh mint leaves, very finely chopped

TO ASSEMBLE

fresh mint leaves, for garnish

COATING

1. Melt the chocolate together with the other coating ingredients, either using the double boiler method (see page 225) or in the microwave.

FILLING

1. Combine the filling ingredients in a bowl and mix using a small hand whisk or electric blender. Transfer the filling to a very small saucepan set over low heat and cook, stirring constantly, until creamy. Remove from the heat, stir in the remaining mint leaves and allow to cool for a few minutes.

TO ASSEMBLE

1. For the chocolate coating, cut a piece of parchment paper about 7 inches (18 cm) square. Place the paper on a 6-inch (15-cm) square plate or other flat, square surface of about the same size (like a Tupperware lid). Make sure the paper is slightly larger than the plate so it will catch any chocolate that falls off.

2. Coat the parchment paper with half the melted chocolate, spreading it evenly. Place in the freezer for 15 minutes, or until solid.

3. With a spatula, spread the minted filling evenly over the chocolate layer, and return to the freezer for another 15 minutes or so, until firm to the touch.

4. Spread the remaining chocolate overtop—do this gently in order not to agitate the filling mixture, in case it has not yet fully set. Garnish with extra mint leaves and cut another piece of parchment paper to place loosely on top. Return to the freezer for another 15–20 minutes, then refrigerate.

5. Remove the parchment paper and use a sharp knife to cut into squares, triangles or whatever shapes you fancy. Serve in a colorful, shallow bowl and enjoy!

NOTE: **Peppermint oil can be found in natural food stores and natural pharmacies. It's very concentrated, so a few drops are all you need.**

DECADENT CHEESES & DAIRY ALTERNATIVES

HAPPY MILK MAKES 4 CUPS (1 L)

THIS HAS GOT TO BE ONE OF THE BEST VEGAN MILKS IN THE WORLD. It's white as snow, smooth, creamy, nutritious and, of course, cholesterol- and cruelty-free. Drink it as is with crushed ice, or use in smoothies and milkshakes or as a milk substitute in any recipe. You can also make a luscious cream substitute by using half the amount of water (see below).

just under ⅔ cup (160 mL) whole cashews, plus water to cover

3 cups (750 mL) cold water

2 tsp (10 mL) agave or maple syrup

1. Place the cashews in a bowl and cover with water. Cover the bowl and leave to soak for a couple of hours in the fridge, or overnight if you wish.

2. Drain the nuts and place them in a food processor with 1 cup (250 mL) of the water. Process for a minute or so.

3. Add the agave and the second cup (250 mL) of water, and process for another 30 seconds.

4. Add the last cup of water, and process for 1–2 minutes.

5. Pour into a jug with a lid and refrigerate, or serve immediately over crushed ice.

6. Use as you would any other nondairy milk. It will stay fresh in the refrigerator for 3–4 days.

VARIATION: HAPPY CREAM

Follow the recipe as directed, except use only 1½ cups (375 mL) water when processing. This makes a rich, thick liquid suitable for any recipes (savory or sweet) that call for cream.

MAYO FROM THE HEAVENS

MAKES ABOUT 1 ½ CUPS (375 ML)

THIS IS THE BEST VEGAN MAYO DRESSING EVER. In fact, it's the best mayo ever, period—vegan or not. It's rich and creamy, but without the excess fat of most ready-made brands. It can be used as a spread on sandwiches and burgers, or you can make a thinner version to use as a dressing for salad and coleslaw—either way, it is truly awesome.

3 Tbsp (45 mL) tahini

2 Tbsp (30 mL) maple or agave syrup

1 Tbsp (15 mL) flaxseed oil

½ tsp (2 mL) hot prepared mustard

3–4 Tbsp (45–60 mL) apple cider vinegar

¾ cup (185 mL) firm silken tofu

¼ tsp (1 mL) smoked paprika

salt to taste

1. Place the tahini, maple syrup, flaxseed oil, mustard and half the vinegar in a small bowl or glass jar, and mix with a teaspoon into a thick paste.

2. Pour the mixture into a medium bowl and add the remaining ingredients.

3. Using a handheld immersion blender, blend until completely smooth. Taste and add more salt and vinegar, if needed.

4. Store in a covered jar in the refrigerator for up to 3 days.

NOTE: **To use as a dressing, add a little extra cold water at the end, a little at a time, mixing vigorously with a fork, until the mixture reaches the consistency you desire.**

VEGAN MOZZARELLA

MAKES 3 CUPS (750 ML), GRATED

OF THE MANY CHEESE VARIETIES I HAVE ATTEMPTED, this has got to be the most versatile and simple to make. A mild cheese that melts beautifully, it's ideal for making panini, pizzas, grilled cheese, mac and cheese, and a host of other recipes. It's great for sandwiches too—try it with avocado, thinly sliced tomatoes, basil and Mayo from the Heavens (see the recipe on page 250).

---

2 cups (500 mL) thick Happy Milk (see page 249—make recipe using only ⅓ the amount of water)

1 cup (250 mL) vegan cream (see page 249 or use purchased)

¼ cup (60 mL) canola or olive oil

2 tsp (10 mL) apple cider vinegar

1 tsp (5 mL) salt

4 Tbsp (60 mL) nutritional yeast

½ tsp (2 mL) fine garlic granules (or less if you wish)

2 Tbsp (30 mL) agar powder (not flakes)

½ tsp (2 mL) agave or maple syrup

1. Lightly grease a small glass bowl, about 5.5 inches (14 cm) in diameter. Set aside.

2. Combine all the ingredients in a blender and process for 1 minute. Taste and add more salt if needed, then process for another minute, until it's nice and smooth.

3. Pour into a saucepan set over medium heat and cook, stirring constantly with a hand whisk, until smooth and thick, about 3–4 minutes (or a little longer if needed).

4. Remove from the heat, allow to cool for 20 minutes, then spoon into the prepared bowl. Allow to cool for another 30 minutes, then cover and refrigerate for a few hours, preferably overnight, or until set.

5. Slice or grate and use in your favorite recipes. The cheese will keep for up to 1 week in the fridge.

NOTE: **For a better melting effect, shred the cheese with a grater, and drizzle a little oil on top before you grill or bake it.**

MILD CHEDDAR "CHEESE"

MAKES ONE 3½- x 4½- x 1½-INCH (9- x 11- x 4-CM) BLOCK

THIS IS A MARVELOUS, mild vegan cheddar that grates beautifully. It melts well, and tastes great in virtually any dish that requires cheese. All that, and it's very simple to make. Ideal for sandwiches, salads, lasagna, mac and cheese, and much more.

2 cups (500 mL) Happy Cream (see page 249 or use purchased)

½ cup (125 mL) olive or coconut oil

2 tsp (10 mL) apple cider vinegar

1 tsp (5 mL) salt

4–5 Tbsp (60–75 mL) nutritional yeast (you can use the lesser amount if the milk is very creamy)

1 tsp (5 mL) onion powder

½ tsp (2 mL) fine garlic granules

1½ Tbsp (22.5 mL) agar powder (not flakes)

¼ tsp (1 mL) turmeric

½ tsp (2 mL) agave or maple syrup

1. Lightly grease a Tupperware (or similar) container, about 3½ x 4½ inches (9 x 11 cm). Set aside.

2. Combine all the ingredients in a food processor and process for a minute or so. Taste and add more salt if needed, then process for another minute.

3. Pour the mixture into a saucepan set over medium heat. Cook for 3–4 minutes, stirring constantly, until smooth and thick.

4. Remove from the heat and allow to cool for 20 minutes, then spoon into the prepared container. Allow to cool for another 30 minutes, then cover and refrigerate for at least a few hours, or overnight. The cheese is then ready to use. It will keep in the fridge for up to 1 week.

NOTE: **When using this to make grilled cheese (see photo on page 263) or in baked dishes, grate it, then drizzle some olive oil on top before baking or grilling. This way, it will remain moist and succulent.**

VARIATION: MILD CHEDDAR SPREAD

For a spreadable cheese, follow the recipe as instructed, but use only 1 Tbsp (15 mL) of agar powder.

MATURE CHEDDAR "CHEESE"

MAKES ONE 4- x 5- x 1-INCH (10- x 12- x 2.5-CM) BLOCK

NONDAIRY CHEESE IS IN GROWING DEMAND, and not just by vegans. It's also ideal for those with lactose intolerance or high cholesterol. And unlike many vegan cheese recipes, this one is very easy to make, with no compromise on flavor. It hits the mark on a "cheese" plate with crackers, with fresh bread or in grilled cheese sandwiches.

1 cup (250 mL) raw cashews

1½ cups (375 mL) water

4 Tbsp (60 mL) olive or coconut oil

1 tsp (5 mL) onion powder

½ tsp (2 mL) fine garlic granules

1 tsp (5 mL) yeast extract (such as Marmite) or miso paste

2 Tbsp (30 mL) apple cider vinegar

2 tsp (10 mL) salt

5 Tbsp (75 mL) nutritional yeast

1 Tbsp + ¾ tsp (20 mL) agar powder (not flakes)—use 1½ Tbsp (22.5 mL) if you prefer a harder cheese

¼ tsp (1 mL) turmeric

2 Tbsp (30 mL) lager or other beer

2½ Tbsp (37.5 mL) cornmeal

1. Grease a small Tupperware (or similar) container, about 4 x 5 inches (10 x 12 cm), and set aside.

2. Combine all the ingredients except the cornmeal in a blender. Blend until you have a nice, smooth liquid with no nut bits—this may take a few minutes.

3. Taste and add more salt if needed—dairy cheese has a lot of salt in it, and this vegan cheddar should match the saltiness and sharpness of a mature cheddar cheese.

4. Add the cornmeal and process for another 10 seconds.

5. Pour the mixture into a saucepan set over low heat. Cook, whisking constantly, for a few minutes, until the mixture is very thick. Remove from the heat and allow to cool.

6. Once mixture has cooled, spoon it into the prepared container. Refrigerate overnight before serving. This cheese will keep in the fridge for up to 1 week.

NOTE: **To use this cheese in grilled cheese or baked dishes, grate it first, then drizzle olive oil on top before cooking. This way, it will remain moist and succulent.**

VARIATION: MATURE CHEDDAR SPREAD

For a spreadable cheese, follow the recipe as instructed, but use only 1 Tbsp (15 mL) of agar powder.

BETA FETA

THIS CHEESE IS A REVELATION IN VEGAN CUISINE. The texture is somewhere between feta, halloumi and cream cheese—it's moist, yet it slices well. And the flavor is incredibly yummy: the combination of olive oil, lemon and herbs lifts it to another level. You can chop up this versatile cheese to add to a Greek salad, or eat it with bread drizzled with olive oil. It can also be used in Middle Eastern dishes or any recipes that call for feta cheese.

1⅓ cups (330 mL) raw cashews, presoaked for a couple of hours

1 heaped Tbsp (about 17 mL) nutritional yeast

1½ tsp (7.5 mL) salt

1 cup (250 mL) water

juice of ½ lemon

1 tsp (5 mL) apple cider vinegar

2 Tbsp (30 mL) olive oil, plus more for drizzling

1 heaped tsp (7 mL) agar powder, mixed into a paste with 3 Tbsp (45 mL) hot water

1 Tbsp (15 mL) chopped fresh dill (optional)

2 Tbsp (30 mL) chopped fresh cilantro (optional)

1 Tbsp (15 mL) chopped mint (optional)

1. Preheat the oven to 350°F (180°C). Grease a small oven-proof dish, about 6½ x 5 inches (15.5 x 12 cm), and line with parchment paper. Set aside.

2. Drain the nuts and place them in a food processor or blender along with the nutritional yeast and salt. Pulse for a few seconds.

3. Add the water little by little, pulsing between each addition, and scraping down the sides with a spatula as often as needed.

4. Keep pulsing until you have a thickish consistency, and taste to ensure the texture is totally smooth—be patient, it will happen.

5. Add the lemon, vinegar and oil and process for a few minutes. Add the agar paste and whizz the mixture for another minute. Taste and add more salt if needed.

6. Spoon the mixture into the prepared dish and distribute the dill (if using) overtop. Flatten the top with a spatula, then drizzle on a little olive oil.

7. Bake in the preheated oven for about 40 minutes, until golden on top. Remove from the oven and allow to cool, then drizzle with a little more olive oil and garnish with the cilantro and mint (if using).

8. When the cheese has cooled completely, cover the dish and place it in the fridge for at least several hours, or overnight. Your cheese is now ready to use. It will keep in the fridge for up to 1 week.

NOTE: **Don't skimp on the salt in this recipe—otherwise it won't work. You can experiment with other fresh herbs in place of the dill, cilantro and mint.**

SWISS VEGAN FONDUE SERVES 4

SHARING A FONDUE WAS ALWAYS A FAVORITE SOCIAL OCCASION FOR ME—a wonderfully collective and intimate experience to share with close friends or family. A lot of fun, too, particularly on a cold winter's evening. This was an experience I wasn't willing to give up, and therefore I needed a vegan version. Serve the fondue with French baguettes cut into bite-sized pieces to dunk into the mixture, and a variety of colorful raw vegetables. Delicious—but you may not have a clean table by the end of the evening!

---

1 clove garlic, cut in half

1 cup (250 mL) raw cashews

1½ cups (375 mL) water

4 Tbsp (60 mL) olive or coconut oil

1 tsp (5 mL) onion powder

½ tsp (2 mL) fine garlic granules

1 tsp (5 mL) yeast extract (such as Marmite) or miso paste

2 Tbsp (30 mL) apple cider vinegar

2 tsp (10 mL) salt

5 Tbsp (75 mL) nutritional yeast

1 Tbsp + 2 tsp (25 mL) cornstarch

a pinch of turmeric, for color

¼ cup (60 mL) white wine

1. Rub the cut garlic clove around the inside of your fondue pot, then discard the garlic.

2. Combine the remaining ingredients except the wine in a blender and blend until you have a nice, smooth liquid with no nut bits. This may take a few minutes.

3. Place the fondue pot over low heat and pour in the white wine. Heat until the wine is warmed, then add the cashew mixture. Whisk until it thickens. Keep the fondue over low heat while you serve it.

4. Now it's time to indulge! Get some chunks of bread and cut-up vegetables, and dig in.

NOTE: **You will need a fondue pot for this recipe.**

NUTTY PARMESAN MAKES ABOUT ½ CUP (125 ML)

THIS HEALTHFUL COMBINATION OF CASHEWS, almonds and nutritional yeast makes an excellent substitute for grated Parmesan cheese in pasta dishes, or wherever you want a "cheesy" flavor. Nutritional yeast is high in vitamin B12, which is difficult to obtain from vegan sources, so this is a good way to make it a regular part of your diet.

½ cup (125 mL) mixed raw cashews and almonds

2 Tbsp (30 mL) nutritional yeast

1 tsp (5 mL) garlic powder

a little salt to taste

1. Combine all the ingredients in a food processor and process until very finely ground.

2. Use in place of grated Parmesan cheese. Store leftovers in a covered container in the refrigerator for up to 1 week.

BÉCHAMEL SAUCE MAKES 4 CUPS (1 L)

HERE IS A VEGAN VERSION OF THE CLASSIC WHITE SAUCE—just as delicious and rich-tasting, but without the cholesterol and saturated fat. It's excellent for topping vegan roasts or vegetables.

5 Tbsp (75 mL) vegan margarine

4 Tbsp (60 mL) unbleached all-purpose flour

4 cups (1 L) nondairy milk (see page 249 or use purchased)

2 tsp (10 mL) salt

½ tsp (2 mL) freshly grated nutmeg

1. Melt the margarine in a medium saucepan set over low heat.

2. Add the flour and stir until smooth. Cook over medium heat until the mixture turns a light golden color, about 6–7 minutes.

3. In the meantime, heat the milk in a separate saucepan, to just before boiling point.

4. Add the hot milk to the margarine mixture a cup at a time, whisking continuously until very smooth.

5. Bring to a boil, then lower the heat and cook for another 10 minutes, stirring constantly.

6. Remove from the heat, stir in the salt and nutmeg, and use immediately. Leftover sauce will keep in the fridge for 1–2 days.

WHY VEGAN?

Twenty years ago, many people had never even heard the word "vegan." Today, veganism is a growing movement that's hard to ignore. People of all ages and backgrounds are converting to vegan diets in increasing numbers, or making the effort to eat meat- and dairy-free meals at least part of the time, often in a quest to better their health. New vegan products, restaurants and stores are popping up every day, in both urban and rural areas. And veganism is a hot topic in the media, with best-selling books and high-profile advocates. Making the decision to turn vegan is the start of an enormously exciting, enriching and rewarding journey. It involves a total shift in awareness and consciousness that infiltrates every aspect of life. Once you turn vegan, it is quite impossible to view things in the same way again.

Vegetarianism can be traced back to the ancient Greek philosophers Pythagoras, Plato and Plutarch, and to the Buddha in India. More recently, in the mid-19th century there was a significant development with the formation of the Vegetarian Society in England in 1847 and the American Vegetarian Society in 1850. This growing movement was closely linked to social reforms. It came about, in part, to provide the poor with an affordable and nutritionally adequate alternative to meat, which many could not afford. Beneath this economic incentive also lay strong ethical and moral reasons for not consuming the meat of other living creatures. As the movement evolved, some vegetarians took its principles a step farther. They believed the consumption or use of any animal products or by-products was in itself exploitation. In 1944, Donald Watson coined the term "vegan" to describe vegetarians who consumed no dairy or eggs. Watson cofounded the Vegan Society, established in London that same year.

Broadly speaking, vegans have been traditionally split into two main categories. Ethical vegans reject the use of animal products or by-products for any purpose, and oppose the perception of animals as a commodity. Dietary vegans, as the name suggests, choose to exclude animal products from their diet, usually for health reasons (see vegan nutrition on page xii).

A third, more recent strand is environmental veganism, which addresses the damage caused by animal production in terms of pollution and the strain on natural resources such as land, water and fossil fuels. In 2006, a UN Food and Agriculture Organization report found industrialized agriculture to "contribute on a 'massive scale' to climate change, air pollution, land degradation, energy use, deforestation, and biodiversity decline."[2] The report, *Livestock's Long Shadow*, found that "the livestock sector (primarily cows, chickens, and pigs) was one of the two or three most significant contributors to the planet's most serious environmental problems, at every scale from local to global . . . it is responsible for at least 18 percent of the world's greenhouse gas emissions, as measured in CO_2 equivalents." What conclusion can we draw from this? By becoming vegan we can reduce our footprint on the planet, and help to preserve it.

Ethical veganism is strongly associated with the concept of animal rights. It has been discussed and defined by a number of academics, including rights theorist Tom Regan, professor emeritus of philosophy at North Carolina State University. Professor Regan argues in favor of veganism "because animals have beliefs and desires—an emotional life, memory, and the ability to initiate action in pursuit of goals—they possess inherent value as 'subjects-of-a-life,' and therefore must be viewed as ends in themselves, not a means to an end."[3] Gary L. Francione, professor of law at Rutgers School of Law–Newark, continues this argument when he writes that "all sentient beings should have at least one right—the right not to be treated as property," and that "adopting veganism must be the unequivocal baseline for anyone who sees nonhuman animals as having intrinsic moral value; to fail to do so is like arguing for human rights while continuing to own human slaves." He also lays bare the ethical argument for veganism when he says, "There is no coherent difference between eating meat and eating dairy or eggs; animals used in the dairy and egg industries live longer, are treated worse, and end up in the same slaughterhouses."[4]

Many people are now aware of the industrialized farming methods used to meet the demand for meat and dairy products in the Western world. For years, multinational food chains have squeezed farmers and food producers to supply meat and dairy products at increasingly low prices, which forces farmers to use more ruthless methods in their quest for super-efficiency. These farming methods pay little or no heed to the welfare and well-being of the animals, who are routinely subjected to a lifetime's confinement in indoor sheds (with no daylight, decent air quality or exercise); to injuries and social stress caused by overcrowding; to health problems and infection; to debeaking (in the poultry industry) to avoid pecking; to force-feeding; to sleeping in their own feces; and much worse. Milk is produced by artificially impregnating cows, which are kept in a constant state of pregnancy in order to lactate, and which have their calves taken away a few days after giving birth to be slaughtered for veal or raised to be dairy cows. Male chicks of egg-laying hens are killed in huge numbers (often gassed or ground alive), since they can't lay eggs themselves. The slaughterhouses are a subject entirely to themselves, but as Sir Paul McCartney has so rightly stated, "If slaughterhouses had glass walls, everyone would be a vegetarian."

> Meatless diets are not just a fad. In fact, some of the most notable artists and thinkers in history are thought to have been vegetarian or vegan, including:
>
> • Pythagoras • Socrates • Plato • Leonardo da Vinci • John Milton • Sir Isaac Newton • Alexander Pope • Voltaire • Benjamin Franklin • Percy Bysshe Shelley • Mary Shelley • Ralph Waldo Emerson • Charles Darwin • Abraham Lincoln • Leo Tolstoy • George Bernard Shaw • Albert Einstein • Gandhi

When we eat, we absorb the entirety of what we eat. Whether it is an animal- or plant-based product, the quality of food is determined by the conditions in which it was reared or grown. If animals are kept in poor conditions, lead a miserable, stressed existence or are force-fed cheap food or given growth hormones, it stands to reason that they are not likely to produce good-quality meat, eggs or milk. This pain and suffering is contained within the food we consume. The same applies to crops grown in poor-quality or contaminated soil, deprived of sun, water and/or enriching nutrients.

Many celebrities have embraced a vegan diet, including

• TV host Ellen DeGeneres • President Bill Clinton • Boxer Mike Tyson • Athlete Carl Lewis • Actors Woody Harrelson, Alec Baldwin, Sandra Oh and Tobey Maguire • Musicians Alanis Morrissette, Bryan Adams, kd lang, Moby and Chrissie Hynde

So it follows that more consumers are choosing animal products labeled "free range," "organic" or "natural." I ask you to be cautious, as such labels can be misleading, and are no guarantee of a good quality of life for animals. Even on smaller-scale operations where farmers may have the best of intentions, animals suffer painful procedures, are often transported on long journeys, in crowded conditions, and end up in the same slaughterhouses as factory-farmed animals. While organic animal products may be better for you—as they contain no antibiotics or hormones—eating a vegan diet as much as possible is without a doubt the most humane choice for animals.

The harm caused to animals during the food production process was one of the main reasons behind my decision to become vegan. We live in a world where it is often hard to find the truth beneath marketing claims, and it is little wonder that many people are ill-informed about the origins of their food, dutifully following the marketeers' strategy as they are guided around the scrupulously planned retail aisles.

I firmly believe that each of us should take responsibility for our food choices, using the tools at our disposal to educate ourselves. Each of us has a moral barometer and, hopefully, a capacity for compassion. I had my own gut reaction to the issues surrounding eating animals and animal products, but I also knew I needed to be fully equipped and informed before making the transition from vegetarian to vegan. In my research, I found organizations, films and speakers that illuminate vegan issues, including People for the Ethical Treatment of Animals (PETA) and the movies *Earthlings* and *Food, Inc.*, as well as Sir Paul McCartney's PETA short, *Glass Walls*. Most influential for me was discovering the powerful animal rights activist Gary Yourofsky, who tirelessly tours universities and colleges through his organization Animals Deserve Absolute Protection Today and Tomorrow (ADAPTT). Gary passionately educates students on all aspects of veganism, leaving behind a trail of newly converted vegans. His compelling lecture on veganism has gained legendary status.[5] An excellent starting point for any would-be vegan, Gary's lecture has even shocked die-hard meat-eaters into instant veganism.

I hope this book will be an exciting and rewarding part of your vegan journey, whether you're at the beginning of your exploration or a seasoned traveler. I invite you to stop by the Mouthwatering Vegan blog (www.mouthwateringvegan.com) or find the Mouthwatering Vegan Recipes page on Facebook to leave a comment, ask a question or share the results of your own adventures in the kitchen.

NOTES

1. American Dietetic Association, Dietitians of Canada, "Position of the American Dietetic Association and Dietitians of Canada: Vegetarian Diets." www.ncbi.nlm.nih.gov/pubmed/12826028
2. Food and Agriculture Organization of the United Nations, "Livestock's Long Shadow: Environmental Issues and Options."www.fao.org/docrep/010/a0701e/a0701e00.HTM
3. Tom Regan, *The Case for Animal Rights*. University of California Press, 1983, p. 243.
4. Gary Francione and Robert Garner, *The Animal Rights Debate: Abolition or Regulation*. Columbia University Press, 2010, p. 62ff.
5. www.adaptt.org/videos.html

ACKNOWLEDGMENTS

Robert McCullough, my publisher, for believing in me and my work, and for being supportive throughout the long journey from concept to completion. His warm heart, enduring optimism, practicality, vision and sense of humor were priceless attributes during the making of this book. I couldn't have asked for a better publisher.

Lindsay Paterson, for her efficiency and patience at all times, and for her willingness to listen, sense of perspective, level head and refreshingly dry Scottish wit.

Paula Ayer, my editor and fellow vegan, who crossed the t's and dotted the i's and saw things through a much-needed vegan lens—thank you for your efficiency and communication.

Eva Veliotou at Evthokia (www.evthokia.co.uk) for her unique "bitten" plate, featured in my photos.

Jonathan, my partner, without whom, frankly, this book would not have happened. He has tirelessly prepared all my manuscripts, liaised throughout with my publisher and editor, kept track of all my material, and handled all the administration and business.

Zara, my dear little daughter, who had to make do without me by her side when the cake almost got burnt, or while I was trying to remember the ingredients for a curry I had just created. She possesses incredible patience for someone so young.

My faithful MWV tribe on Facebook: Kathleen Canfield, Linda Camac, Phil Stewart, McKenna Grace Fisher, Michael Harrison, Staci-lee Sherwood, Eddie Mah, Nina Frangieh and Cindy Metzger Nielsen, to name but a few. Thanks as well to the Vegan Society, and all the wonderful people who preordered a copy of my book many, many months in advance of its sale. I am lucky and grateful to have such supportive people in my life. To my special friends in Malta—Mario and Olga—for their personal support. Thanks also to my special friend, Ian Morrison, who has been a solid rock and very special on this journey—always there over the years and reliable as ever. And to my very best and long-standing friend Mario Attard—such a creative and supportive inspiration, an uplifting tonic, and the soulmate with whom I have shared my highest and lowest moments.

Finally, a big thanks to you, the reader, for picking up this book and trying some of my recipes. It's only through you that we can spread the joy of healthful, compassionate cooking and eating!

INDEX